Transcultural Picture Word List: Vol. II

Judy P. Donaldson
ESL Program Coordinator
(English as Second Language)
Granite School District, Utah

For
Teaching English To Children
From Any of Twelve
Language Backgrounds

LP **Learning Publications, Inc.**

Learning Publications, Inc.
P.O. Box 1326
Holmes Beach, Florida 33509

Designed by Rob Gutek

Library of Congress Catalog Card Number 78-58532

Paperback: ISBN 0-918452-38-4

Printing: 1 2 3 4 5 6 7 8   Year: 3 4 5 6 7 8

Printed in the United States of America

ACKNOWLEDGEMENT

This book is dedicated to those involved in the vital process of language learning with its complex cultural implications and to their teachers in the belief that communication among the peoples of the earth is all-important to a peaceful universe.

I wish to express my deep gratitude and sincere appreciattion to each of you, wherever you may be, for the time and effort you have so generously given for the purpose of helping us to communicate more easily and to further the cause of brotherhood, love and understanding.

Without your help, this work would not have been accomplished.

J.P.D.

FOREWORD

The following information is included for the purpose of advising the reader regarding the scope, intent, and interpretation of the Syntax Variations, Dolch Word Lists, and use of the Word Pairs.

Syntax Variations are designed to enable the reader to understand in a basic way, how English and the other languages compare. The comparison regards word order in sentences, and in some cases the use or omission of various parts of speech. Alphabet comparisons and pronounciations are close approximations due to many varying factors too numerous to list.

Most definitions, as translated in the *Dolch Word Lists,* are written at an elementary grade level. With all words more easily understood, students at all grade levels will be able to make maximum use of the word lists.

Word Pairs are included to help identify the individual who is having phonological interference with English and the native language. When a person has this problem, he or she will have difficulty determining whether the word pairs sound the "same" or "different." This problem is common with persons who are still "hearing" in their native language.

TABLE OF CONTENTS

Introduction

The Transcultural Picture Word List, with more than 600 entries, was created for the purpose of helping teachers to help the students who have English as a second language, to learn English more rapidly and at the same time, reinforce the knowledge of their native language.

Letters to the parents are included in the various languages, so that the parents can reinforce, at home, what the students are being taught in school; this will minimize fragmented learning by allowing the vocabulary of the students to be built on concrete knowledge of the words in both languages, based on the premise that a person can only utilize a vocabulary that he understands. This will help to narrow the degree of difference between the student's oral and silent reading comprehension level.

Information on the syntax variants and letter transpositions, such at "p" for "v", "wif" for "with", etc., are included to give the teacher a synopsis of characteristic difficulties that students of a specific language background, that is different from English, may exhibit. This information is given with the hope that a teacher who is prepared, in advance, to meet the learning difficulties of students, may help to make the acquisition of English a pleasant experience.

The next four sections of the book contain basic transcultural picture word lists of things (nouns), opposites, place or position (near-far), actions, colors, numbers and shapes with the English word for the object, action, etc. printed under the picture.

The final section of the book is made up of the *220 Basic Sight Word List** by Edward W. Dolch in the various languages. The list, when learned, will serve as a springboard into more rapid progress in your reading program.

Flashcards, in any languages, can be made, either from the "Dolch List," and/or from the various entries found in *The Transcultural Picture Word List*. The teacher would make the cards, to assure uniformity of size. The teacher or the student would then write the word in English on one side of the card. The student, or parent, would then write the word in his native language, on the reverse side.

Implementation of these ideas and materials will greatly assist those teachers and schools where a bilingual teacher or program is not possible. Bilingual teachers and their programs can also utilize these ideas and materials as valuable supplements.

---

*Reprinted from Edward W. Dolch, *220 Basic Sight Word List*, by permission of the publisher. (Copyright, Garrard Publishing Company.) The *220 Basic Sight Word List* by Edward W. Dolch is available in card form from the Garrard Publishing Company / 1607 North Market Street / Champaign, Illinois.

SECTION I

Letters to Parents

This section includes letters in the following languages:

Croatian	Indonesian
Czech	Polish
Danish	Portuguese
Finnish	Russian
Hmong & Mong	Swedish
Hungarian	Thai

CROATIAN

Dear Parents of ————————————————— Date ————————————

    Please help the school to be able to help your child learn to read and write in English more easily. At different times during the school year, your child will bring home word lists or pictures with the names of objects written in English and a blank line beside or under them, for you to write the meanings on the blank lines, in your own language. If your child can hear you say the word in your language, and see how it is written, he will be able to understand what the meaning is in English also; and at the same time, be studying his own language. Any help you can give your child will be appreciated.

————————————————————
Teacher

Dragi————————————————Roditelji   Datum————————————

    Molim vas da pomognete školi da pomogne vašem djetetu da lakše nauči čitati i pisati engleski. Tokom školske godine dijete će donositi popise riječi ili slike sa imenima predmeta na engleskom i praznom crtom pored ili ispod njiḥ, da ispunite značenje riječi na vašem jeziku. Kada dijete bude čulo kako izgovarate riječ na vašem jeziku, i vidi kako se ona piše, razumjet će što znači na engleskom; istouremeno će učiti materinji jezik. Zahvalni smo vam za svaku pomoć vašem djetetu.

S poštovanjem

————————————————————
Učitelj

CZECH

Dear Parents of ———————————————————— Date ————————————————

    Please help the school to be able to help your child learn to read and write in English more easily. At different times during the school year, your child will bring home word lists or pictures with the names of objects written in English and a blank line beside or under them, for you to write the meanings on the blank lines, in your own language. If your child can hear you say the word in your language, and see how it is written, he will be able to understand what the meaning is in English also; and at the same time, be studying his own language. Any help you can give your child will be appreciated.

———————————————————
Teacher

Vážení rodiče ———————————————————— Datum ————————————————

    Prosíme Vás, abyste pomohli škole snadněji naučit Vaše dítě číst a psát anglicky. Vaše dítě bude občas nosit listy se slovíčky nebo obrázky s názvy předmětů v angličtině a vedle nich nebo pod nimi bude prázdná linka, na kterou napíšete český výraz. Jestliže Vaše dítě uslyší jak se předmět čte a píše česky, bude také lépe rozumět jeho významu v angličtině. Současně se tím bude také učit svému rodnému jazyku. Uvítáme každou pomoc, kterou svému dítěti poskytnete.

———————————————————
učitel

DANISH

Dear Parents of _____ Date _____

    Please help the school to be able to help your child learn to read and write in English more easily. At different times during the school year, your child will bring home word lists or pictures with the names of objects written in English and a blank line beside or under them, for you to write the meanings on the blank lines, in your own language. If your child can hear you say the word in your language, and see how it is written, he will be able to understand what the meaning is in English also; and at the same time, be studying his own language. Any help you can give your child will be appreciated.

_____
Teacher

TIL _____ FORAELDRE _____ DATO _____

    VIL DE VAERE SAA VENLIG AT HJELPE OS, SAA DERES BARN KAN LETTERE LAERE AT LAESE OG SKRIVE ENGELSK. IGENNEM SKOLEAARET, VIL DERES BARN BRINGE EN LISTE AF ORD OG BILLEDER HJEM, NAVNENE VIL BLIVE SKREVET PAA ENGELSK, DER VIL OGSAA VAERE EN LINGE HVOR DE KAN SKRIVE ORDET OG MENINGEN AF BILLEDERNE PAA DANSK, PAA DEN MAADE, NAAR DE LAESER DET HOJT, WIL DERES BARN LAERE HVORDAN DET UDTALES, OG VIL SAA VAERE I STAND TIL AT LAERE BEAAE SPROG. VI VIL PAASKONNE ENHVER HJAELP DE KAN GIVE OS.

_____
LAERER

FINNISH

Dear Parents of ———————————————————— Date ————————————————

    Please help the school to be able to help your child learn to read and write in English more easily. At different times during the school year, your child will bring home word lists or pictures with the names of objects written in English and a blank line beside or under them, for you to write the meanings on the blank lines, in your own language. If your child can hear you say the word in your language, and see how it is written, he will be able to understand what the meaning is in English also; and at the same time, be studying his own language. Any help you can give your child will be appreciated.

————————————————————
Teacher

Päiväys:

Arvoisat vanhemmat,

Pyydämme kohteliaimmin apuanne, jotta voisimme auttaa lastanne oppimaan lukemaan ja kirjoittamaan englantia mahdollisimman helposti. Aika ajoittain lukuvuoden aikana lapsenne tuo kotiin sanaluetteloja tai kuvasarjoja, joissa on englanniksi esineitten nimiä sekä tyhjiä rivejä, joille voitte kirjoittaa samat sanat suomeksi. Jos lapsenne voi kuulla teidän sanovan sanan suomeksi ja nähdä, kuinka se kirjoitetaan, hän pystyy ymmärtämään englanninkielisen sanan merkityksen - ja oppii samanaikaisesti suomea. Olemme kiitollia avustanne lapsenne hyväksi.

Kunnioittaen,

————————————
Opettaja

HMONG

Dear Parents of ———————————————————— Date ————————————————

Please help the school to be able to help your child learn to read and write in English more easily. At different times during the school year, your child will bring home word lists or pictures with the names of objects written in English and a blank line beside or under them, for you to write the meanings on the blank lines, in your own language. If your child can hear you say the word in your language, and see how it is written, he will be able to understand what the meaning is in English also; and at the same time, be studying his own language. Any help you can give your child will be appreciated.

———————————————————————
Teacher

Nyob zoo txog niam txiv ntawm ————————————— tim ————————————————

Thov pab koom tes nrog tseem fwv (xwb fwb) los yog kws qhia ntawv, kom muaj cuab kav pab nej cov me nyuam, kawm nyeem thiab sau ntawv askiv (English) yooj yim. Nyob rau hauv lub sij hawm txawv txav nrab xyoo kawm ntawv ntawd, nej cov me nyuam yuav nqa ntawv (tsiaj ntawv) los yog duab uas muaj npe sau nrog.los ua npe ntawv askiv thiab tseg tej kab kos nrog, uas nyob ib sab los yog hauv qab ntawd los tsev. Cia rau nej sau yam tseeb ntsiab rau ntawm txoj kab kos ua nej yam lus. yog li, nej me nyuam hnov nej hais cov lus ntawd ua nej yam lus thiab ho pom tias sau li cas ntawd, nws yuav muaj cuab kav nkag siab thoob tsib yam ntawd hauv ntawv askiv tib yam; thiab sij hawm ua ke ntawd, yuav muaj cuab kav kawm tau nws yam lus nrog. Txhia yam pab cuam uas nej muaj cuab kav ua pab rau nej cov me nyuam, kuj muaj lus zoo siab kawg.

———————————————————————
KWS QHIA NTAWV

MONG

Dear Parents of _____ Date _____

Please help the school to be able to help your child learn to read and write in English more easily. At different times during the school year, your child will bring home word lists or pictures with the names of objects written in English and a blank line beside or under them, for you to write the meanings on the blank lines, in your own language. If your child can hear you say the word in your language, and see how it is written, he will be able to understand what the meaning is in English also; and at the same time, be studying his own language. Any help you can give your child will be appreciated.

_____

Teacher

Nyob zoo txug nam txiv ntawm _____ tim _____

Thov paab koom teg nrug tseem fwv (xwb fwb) los yog kws qha ntawv, kuas muaj cuab kaav paab mej cov miv nyuad, kawm nyeem hab sau ntawv aaskiv (English) yooj yim. Nyob rua huv lub noob nyoog txawv txaav nraab xyoo kawm ntawv ntawd, mej cov miv nyuad yuav nqaa ntawv (tsaj ntawv) los yog dluab kws muaj npe sau nrug lug ua npe ntawv aaskiv, hab tseg tej kaab kus nrug, kws nyob ib saab ntawd los yog huv qaab lug tsev. Ca rua mej sau yaam tseeb ntsab rua ntawm txuj kaab kus; ua mej yaam lug. Yog le, mej tug miv nyuad nov mej has los yog nyeem cov lug ntawd ua mej yaam lug hab ho pum tas sau le caag ntawd, nwg yuav muaj peev xwm nkaag sab thoob tsib yaam ntawd huv ntawv aaskiv tuab yaam; Hab noob nyoog ua ke ntawd yuav muaj cuab kaav kawm tau nwg yaam lug nrug. Txua yaam paab cuam kws mej muaj cuab kaav ua paab rua mej cov miv nyuad, kuj muaj lug zoo sab kawg.

_____

KWS QHA NTAWV

HUNGARIAN

Dear Parents of ———————————————— Date ————————————

Please help the school to be able to help your child learn to read and write in English more easily. At different times during the school year, your child will bring home word lists or pictures with the names of objects written in English and a blank line beside or under them, for you to write the meanings on the blank lines, in your own language. If your child can hear you say the word in your language, and see how it is written, he will be able to understand what the meaning is in English also; and at the same time, be studying his own language. Any help you can give your child will be appreciated.

————————————————
Teacher

Kedves Szülök ———————————————— Dátum————————————

Segítségüket szeretnénk kérni abban, hogy gyermekeik minél könnyebben megtanuljanak irni és olvasni. Az iskola év folyamán gyermekük idönként egy kép vagy szó listát fog hazavinni amelyen a tárgyak angol neve fog szerepelni, egy üres vonallal alattuk vagy mellettük. Kérjük, hogy irják be a megfelelö szavakat anyanyelvükön. Ha a gyermek hallja a kimondott szót az önök nyelvén és ugyanakkor látja is leirva, az angol jelentést is, megfogja érteni. Emmellett saját nyelvét is tanulni fogja. Hálásan köszönünk minden segítséget, melyet gyermeküknek nyújtani tudnak.

————————————————
Tanár (or) tanárnö

INDONESIAN

Dear Parents of _____ Date _____

    Please help the school to be able to help your child learn to read and write in English more easily. At different times during the school year, your child will bring home word lists or pictures with the names of objects written in English and a blank line beside or under them, for you to write the meanings on the blank lines, in your own language. If your child can hear you say the word in your language, and see how it is written, he will be able to understand what the meaning is in English also; and at the same time, be studying his own language. Any help you can give your child will be appreciated.

                                                    _____

                                                    Teacher

Yang terhormat orang tua dari --------------------------------Tanggal--------

Tolonglah sekolah ini untuk menolong anak saudara membaca dan menulis dalam bahasa$_2$Inggeris dengan lebih mudah. Dalam waktu yang berbeda selama tahun^2 pelajaran sekolah, anak saudara akan membawa pulang daftar kata^2 atau gambar^2 dengan nama^2 yang tertulis dalam bahasa Inggeris dengan garis kosong disamping atau dibawahnja, untuk saudara menulis artinya didalam garis^2 kosong itu, didalam bahasa saudara sendiri. Kalau anak saudara dapat mendengar apa yang saudara katakan dalam bahasa saudara sendiri, dan lihat bagaimana menulisnya, dia akan mengerti juga apa artinya didalam bahasa Inggeris; dan dalam waktu yang sama, belajar dalam bahasanya sendiri. Pertolongan apa saja yang dapat saudara berikan pada anak saudara akan kita hargai.

                                       Guru

POLISH

Dear Parents of _____ Date _____

    Please help the school to be able to help your child learn to read and write in English more easily. At different times during the school year, your child will bring home word lists or pictures with the names of objects written in English and a blank line beside or under them, for you to write the meanings on the blank lines, in your own language. If your child can hear you say the word in your language, and see how it is written, he will be able to understand what the meaning is in English also; and at the same time, be studying his own language. Any help you can give your child will be appreciated.

_____

Teacher

Do Rodziców _____ Data _____

    Szanowni Państwo! Prosimy o udzielenie szkole pomocy w nauczaniu dziecka Państwa lepiej czytać i pisac po angielsku. W trakcie roku szkolnego, dziecko przynosić będzie do domu listy wyrazów lub obrazków z podpisami w języku angielskim. Prosimy bardzo, aby Państwo napisali obok, w swoim slasnym języku, ich znaczenie lub odpowiedniki. Dziecko, slysząc dane slowo wypowiedziane w swoim języku i poznając jego pisownię, latwiej przyswoi sobie jego znaczenie po angielsku, jednocześnie zaz-najamiając się lepiej ze swoim językiem. Będziemy Państwu wdzięczni za wszelką pomoc udzieloną dziecku.

_____

Nauczyciel(ka)

PORTUGUESE

Dear Parents of _____ Date _____

    Please help the school to be able to help your child learn to read and write in English more easily. At different times during the school year, your child will bring home word lists or pictures with the names of objects written in English and a blank line beside or under them, for you to write the meanings on the blank lines, in your own language. If your child can hear you say the word in your language, and see how it is written, he will be able to understand what the meaning is in English also; and at the same time, be studying his own language. Any help you can give your child will be appreciated.

_____
Teacher

Queridos Pais de _____ Data _____

    Por favor ajudem a escola poder ajudar seu filho (sua filha) a aprender a ler e escrever em ingles com facilidade. De vez em quando, durante o ano, seu filho deverá trazerá listas de palavras com os nomes dos objectos escritos em ingles e uma lihna em branco ao lado para voces escreverem o significado nas linhas, na sua própria lingua. Se seu filho puder ouvir dizer a palavra na sua própria língua, e ver como está escrita, poderá entender o significado tambéin em ingles e, ao mesmo tempo, estará estudando a sua própria lingua. Qualquer ajuda que puderem dar a seu filho(a) será apreciada.

Sinceramente,

_____
Professora/Professor

RUSSIAN

Dear Parents of _____ Date _____

Please help the school to be able to help your child learn to read and write in English more easily. At different times during the school year, your child will bring home word lists or pictures with the names of objects written in English and a blank line beside or under them, for you to write the meanings on the blank lines, in your own language. If your child can hear you say the word in your language, and see how it is written, he will be able to understand what the meaning is in English also; and at the same time, be studying his own language. Any help you can give your child will be appreciated.

_____
Teacher

Дорогие родители_____Число_____

Школа просит вашей помощи в обучений Вашего ребёнка лучше писать и читать по-английски. В разное время учебного года Ваш ребёнок будет приносить домой лист со словами или картинками с названиями предметов, написаниями по-английски для того чтобы Вы написали значения этих слов или названия этих предметов на Вашем родном языке. Если ребёнок будет понимать значение слова на родном языке, а также увидит как оно пишется, он сможет понимать значение этого слова и по-английски, не забывая в то же время и своего родного языка.

Любая помощь, какую вы могли бы оказать вашему ребёнку, будет принята с благодарностью.

Учитель_____

SWEDISH

Dear Parents of _____ Date _____

Please help the school to be able to help your child learn to read and write in English more easily. At different times during the school year, your child will bring home word lists or pictures with the names of objects written in English and a blank line beside or under them, for you to write the meanings on the blank lines, in your own language. If your child can hear you say the word in your language, and see how it is written, he will be able to understand what the meaning is in English also; and at the same time, be studying his own language. Any help you can give your child will be appreciated.

_____
Teacher

Kära Föräldrar till _____ Datum _____

Vill ni vara snälla och hjälpa ert barn med skolarbetet så att det lättare kan lära sig skriva och läsa på engelska. Vid olika tillfällen under årets lopp kommer ert barn att ta hem listor eller bilder med namn på olika saker skrivna på engelska, vid sidan om bilden, eller under den, finns en tom rad för dig att skriva detsamma på ert eget språk. Om ert barn hör ordet uttalas på sitt eget språk, och ser det skrivet, så kommer han/hon att förstå vad det är på engelska på samma gång som det studerar sitt eget språk. Vi uppskatar all den hjälp som ni kan ge ert barn.

_____
Lärare/lärarinna

THAI

Dear Parents of _____ Date _____

    Please help the school to be able to help your child learn to read and write in English more easily. At different times during the school year, your child will bring home word lists or pictures with the names of objects written in English and a blank line beside or under them, for you to write the meanings on the blank lines, in your own language. If your child can hear you say the word in your language, and see how it is written, he will be able to understand what the meaning is in English also; and at the same time, be studying his own language. Any help you can give your child will be appreciated.

_____
Teacher

เรียน   ท่านผู้ปกครอง _____ ทราบ วันที่ _____

ทางโรงเรียนขอความร่วมมือจากท่านช่วยให้เด็ก เรียนอ่านเขียนภาษาอังกฤษง่ายขึ้น   โดยบางครั้งเด็ก ของท่านอาจจะนำรายชื่อหรือรูปภาพของสิ่งของ ซึ่งจะมี ชื่อเป็นภาษาอังกฤษเขียนกำกับ   และมีช่องว่างเว้นใกล้ๆ หรือใต้คำศัพท์สำหรับให้ท่านเขียน คำแปลเป็นภาษาไทย ในช่องว่างนั้น   ถ้าเด็กได้ฟังและเรียนเขียนในภาษาของ ตัวเอง ก็จะช่วยให้เข้าใจทั้งสอง ภาษาไปด้วยในตัว   ขอ ขอบคุณในความร่วมมือเพื่อช่วยให้เด็กของท่านเข้าใจ ภาษายิ่งขึ้น

_____
ครูประจำชั้น

SECTION II
Explanation of Syntax Variants

This section includes explanations for the following languages:

Croatian	Indonesian
Czech	Polish
Danish	Portuguese
Finnish	Russian
Hmong & Mong	Swedish
Hungarian	Thai

LINGUISTIC INTERFERENCE WITH
CROATIAN, SERBIAN, AND YUGOSlAV/ENGLISH

Syntax Variants

> English:　I see the black dog.
> Croatian:　See black dog.

There are no articles (a, the) in Croatian, and they are often dropped or omitted. Pronouns are built into verbs, and are dropped also.

Gender, masculine, feminine or neuter, shows in nouns, pronouns and adjectives. Inanimate things and nature phenomenons are of masculine, feminine or neuter genders: Sea - it (neuter), Mountain - She (feminine), Hill - he (masculine).

Denotations of time and place are placed in the sentence according to their importance to the contex.

> English:　I went to school yesterday.
> Croation:　Yesterday I went to school, or to school I went yesterday, or yesterday to school I went, depending on what the speaker wants to stress.

There are four main Yugoslav languages, they are written in two alphabets: *Latinic* for Croatian and Slovenian, *Cyrilic* for Serbian and Macedonian. These languages have numerous dialects, which vary greatly in vocabulary and pronunciation.

There are mainly two levels of language: *Written* and *spoken.* Spoken language is often a blend of written language and local dialect, or pure dialect.

There is a difference in addressing friends and children and adults and acquaintances or strangers, like in German, (du and sie). In some areas, even parents would be addressed respectfully (sie) and a child would use third person plural when speaking of a parent or teacher. "Them, (my mother) said..."

Irregular verbs present difficulty and have to be memorized and their uses practiced. Since "to have" is not used as an auxiliary verb, there is a tendency to use past tense instead of perfect, "we have been married for years" Yugoslavs would phrase as, "we were married for years", meaning they still are married.

"At" is often used in the meaning of "by" and "in" in the meaning of "at" ("we'll meet at school" would mean somewhere around the building. In Croatian children are "in school" if they are attending classes).

Uses of idioms could be confusing. "I am going down the road" would mean that you going downhill. To "straighten things up," would mean that you will walk or ride to some place in order to do it; the stress would be on the going, not on the doing.

WORD PAIRS

Whale - Veal	Think - Tink
That - Dat	Man - Men
Them - Dem	Bird - Beard
Ship - Sheep	You - Jew
Steam - Stem	
Three - Tree	

In dealing with parents, it would be useful to remember that addressing an adult by first name without his or her permission has been considered rude. However, if a parent addresses a teacher by the first name, he is just trying to apply what strikes him as a particular American habit.

Alphabet sounds in Latinic and Cyrilic are pronounced in the same way.

A - F<u>a</u>st	А, а	(A)
B - <u>B</u>ee	Б, б	(B)
C - TC, Live German Zurich	В, в	(V)
Ć - TJ, fast together, like Italian <u>Chi</u>ao	Г, г	(G)
Č - <u>Ch</u>oke	Д, д	(D)
D - <u>D</u>og	Ђ, ђ	(Đ)
DŽ - <u>J</u>ames, harder	Е, е	(E)
Đ - <u>J</u>ames, softer	Ж, ж	(Ž)
E - P<u>e</u>t	З, з	(Z)
F - Fist	И, и	(i)
G - <u>G</u>rade	Ј, ј	(J)
H - <u>H</u>ut	К, к	(K)
I - Sh<u>i</u>p	Л, л	(L)
J - <u>J</u>uma	Љ, љ	(Lj)
K - <u>C</u>one	М, м	(M)
L - <u>L</u>ake	Н, н	(N)
LJ - LF fast together	Њ, њ	(NJ)
M - <u>M</u>an	О, о	(O)
N - <u>N</u>ice	П, п	(P)
NJ - <u>N</u>ew	Р, р	(R)
O - C<u>o</u>rn	С, с	(S)
P - <u>P</u>en	Т, т	(T)
R - <u>R</u>un, harder	Ћ, ћ	(Ć)
S - <u>S</u>on	У, у	(U)
Š - <u>Sh</u>oe	Ф, ф	(F)
T - <u>T</u>op	Х, х	(H)
U - L<u>oo</u>se	Ц, ц	(C)
V - <u>V</u>eal	Ч, ч	(Č)
Ž - <u>Z</u>ebu	Џ, џ	(DŽ)
Ž - like French Je	Ш, ш	(Š)

Students who can read and write in Cyrilic would be confused about letters V-B, R-P, C-S, X-H, W-V, Y-J. The language is quite phonetic, and every sound has its corresponding letter. For example: "New York" would be spelled as pronounced, "NJU JORK" (j is pronounced as Y), fish as "FIS", Jam as "DEN", city as "SITI", Cat as "KET". Consequently, when learning to read and write, students do not depend on spelling as is done with English. Teacher would dictate "blue" as "B-L-U-E". This makes memorizing the way words are spelled rather easy for a student who has already mastered writing in Croatian. However, small children who have just started to recognize letters and put them together would find English spelling a hindrance when trying to read in Croatian. The principle of "a sound for a letter" makes reading in English rather difficult. While reading, the student would pronounce a sound for every letter, like "New York" as "N-E-V Y-O-R-K" or "fish" as "F-I-S-H", or "Judy, as "J-OO-D-I".

VOWEL AND CONSONANT TRANSPOSITIONS

Pronounciation difficulties arise with voiced and unvoiced th, w, and q which do not exist. There are local dialects in which "h" is not pronounced at the beginning of a word. Students would tend to pronounce (and write) "ard" instead of "hard", "evy" instead of "heavy". There are difficulties with "R" as in "run", which could be much harder and more rolling than in English. Similarly with "J" as in "Jam", which would be pronounced much softer or harder, depending on the student's native dialect. There could be confusion with broad and soft "E" as in "Men" and "Pen", also depending on the native dialect, as well as with long and short I (ship-sheep) or long and short "U" (school-tends to be pronounced in a very short way). Indefinite article "A" (A tree) would be pronounced as in "fast". Voiced and unvoiced "TH" are often pronounced as "D" or "T", with = wid or wit, them = tem or dem.

LINGUISTIC INTERFERENCE WITH
CZECH/ENGLISH

Syntax Variants

English: The old black dog is running down the road.
Czech: Old black dog running down road.

English: I see the black dog.
Czech: See black dog.

The Czech language does not use articles (a, an, the). There are three genders, masculine, feminine and neuter. The letters used at the end of the word indicate the gender as well as person and tense.

BASIC VOWELS

ä as in at
A as in ah (as in father)
E as in eh
I as in ee
O as in saw
U as in school
Y as in feet

DOUBLE VOWELS

IA
IE
IU
Ô
OU

VOWEL AND CONSONANT TRANSPOSITIONS

I = an E sound
O = as AW as in saw
Y = an E sound as in feet
W = V
J = yĕ

ALPHABET PRONOUNCIATION

A = ah (as in father)		I = ee (as in feet)	
B = bā		J = ya	
C = tsay		K = ka	
D = day		L = la	
E = eh		M = ma	
F = eff		N = na	
G = gay		O = as in saw	
H = hah (as in father)		P = pay	
CH = like nacht (in German)		Q = kway	

R = air
Ř = no English translation
S = ess
T = tay
U = oo (as in school)
V = vay
W = dvoy - teh vay
X = iks
Y = ipsilon = $\overline{e}$
Z = zet

CONFUSING BLENDS AND TRANSPOSITIONS

Initial voiced - TH as in the = da, this = dis
Initial unvoiced - TH as in thumb = tum
                   TH as in thank = tank
                   TH as in three = tree
Final Unvoiced - TH as in Teeth = teef or tees
                   Both = boat
Final G and K bag/back, dog/dock

WORD PAIR COMPARISONS

This - Dis	Led - Let
That - Dat	Teeth - Tees
Mother - Mudder	Both - Boat
Winter - Vinter	Both - Bof
Work - Vork	Bag - Back
Bed - Bet	Dock - Dog

LINGUISTIC INTERFERENCE WITH
DANISH/ENGLISH

Syntax Variants

The sentence structure of Danish is practically as in English, however, Danish do not use the form like "is running."

English: The old black dog is running down the road.
Danish: The old black dog runs down the road.
Gender is as in English

DIFFICULT WORD PAIRS

Very - Vary	Just - Yust	Window - Vindow
We - Vee	Teeth - Teet	Thirty - Dirty
Worm - Warm	South - Sout	Through - True
Ship - Sheep	Wish - Vish	

The English "th" sound should not be a problem as it is just like sound in bille<u>de</u>, sø<u>de</u> etc, common Danish words. There are some persons who do have difficulty with the unvoiced "th" as in "teeth = teet", "south = sout" etc.

DANISH ALPHABET

the Danish alphabet has nine (9) vowels and 20 consonants.

A as in ask
B as in begin
C as in celebrate
D as in deliver
E as in enlighten
F as in efficient
G as in gander
H as in hope
I as in infant
J as in joke
K as in corn
L as in elevate
M as in employee
N as in endure
O as in door
P as in pen

Q as in coop
R as in err
S as in estimate
T as in television
U as in do
V as in veteran
W (double v) no Danish words spelled with this letter. Pronounced like world, wine
X as in extra
Y as in physics
Z as in set, zet
Æ equals ae, pronounced like egg
Ö equals oe, pronounced like u in murky
å (formerly aa) as in goal, hall

DANISH VOWELS

A as in b<u>a</u>t
E as in <u>e</u>ternal
I as in <u>ea</u>t
O as in b<u>oo</u>k

U as in d<u>o</u>
Y as in l<u>y</u>mph
Æ as in <u>e</u>gg
Ø or Ö as in b<u>i</u>rd or m<u>u</u>rky

å as in g<u>oa</u>l

LINGUISTIC INTERFERENCE
WITH FINNISH/ENGLISH

Syntax Variants

English:	I see the black dog.
Finnish:	I see black dog. (no articles)
English:	The black old dog is running down the road.
Finnish:	Old black dog runs road down/down road.
English:	Do you sing?
Finnish:	Sing you?
English:	The color of the house is blue.
Finnish:	House's color is blue.

Finnish is an agglutanative language: instead of using prepositions, endings are added to the stem -they are called cases, and there are 14 of them in use currently.

talo (house), talossa (in the house), taloon (into the house), talosta (from the house) etc.
taloni (my house), talosi (your house) etc.

The verbs are conjugated by adding personal ending to the root of the verb:

saan (I get), saat (you get), saa (he gets), saamme (we get) saatte (you get), saavat (they get)

The adjectives must agree with case and number with the noun they modify.

Word Pair Comparisons

wine	-	vine	then	-	ten	zipper	-	sipper
then	-	den	want	-	van	teeth	-	teet
both	-	bof	jeep	-	cheap	shall	-	sal
chair	-	share	bee	-	pea	fat	-	fad
shoes	-	choose	pig	-	pick	big	-	bick
with	-	wit	the	-	da	with	-	wif

Alphabet Pronounciation in Finnish (underlining indicates length)

A	ah	N	en	A	ah
B	ba	O	oh	Ä	a as in hat
C	sa	P	pah	Ö	⋺ as in the)
D	da	Q	koo		
E	ah	R	trilled err		
F	ef	S	es		
G	ga	T	tah		
H	hoh	U	oo		
I	ee	V	vah		
J	yee	W	kaksios-v (pronounced like w)		
K	koh	X	eks		
L	el	Y	euh		
M	em	Z	tset		

All vowels can be doubled - that is, their length is doubled. Vowels can be combined in the following diphthongs:

ai	I	oi	as in boil
ui	oowe	ei	as in bay
äi	ahie	öi	ᴐuie (the first sound like e in the)
yi	euhie	au	as in cow
ou	as in go	eu	aoo
iu	eoo	äy	aoo
uo	oowo	öy	ᴐuh (the first sound like e in the)
ie	eah	yö	euh + (the sound like e in the)

All consonants - except b,c,d,q,x,z - can be doubled - that is, their length is doubled:

kuka = who, kukka = flower

The English sound th /ᴅ , ⊖/,/z/,sh/ *S* /,b,g,j,/ *ʒ* /, and w do not exist in Finnish.

LINGUISTIC INTERFERENCE WITH
HMONG-WHITE, MONG-BLUE/ENGLISH

Syntax Variants

English: I see the black dog.

Hmong: I see the black dog.

There are three tenses for the Hmong language. However, only the present tense is used. Ex: "I go" is used for past, future, present. This morning I go to the store. No use of past tense. Never use was or were. The morning is already gone, so no need for went. Plurals are made by adding a number and using the singular word form: Boys = one boy, two boy, several men = many man. The forms of "to be" are different. Ex: English = (I am, you are) Hmong (I am, you am). The third person also uses am. They am, it am. The word is, is not used. Ex: He sick. He fat. He old.

Direction of reading and writing is left to right. There are seven voice tones or language markings. The use of the following letters at the end of a word denote this: M, S, G, D, V, J, B. Maum, maus, muag, muad, mauv, mauj, maub. The voice tones give meaning and expression to the word. For example, muam = sister, muas = to buy, maug = sale, mauj = have, maub = give.

DIFFICULT BLENDS OR SOUND TRANSPOSITIONS

TH	D/T
R	CH
X	SH
B/P	K/ng

WORD PAIR COMPARISONS

Choose - Shoes	Think - Thing
Bed - Bet	Three - Tree
Pay - Bay	Thought - Though
Wear - Were	Wrist - Rest
Let - Left	Race - Raise
Dot - Dog	Letter - Ledder
Laugh - Leaf	Lift - Left

VOWELS

The vowels are always pronounced the same way:

A as in father	AU = as in out
E as in A in gay	UA = Owa
I as in E in feet	IA = Eya
O as in O in off	AI = i as in nice
U as in O in do	AW = er as in father
W = oo as in flu	EE = ing as in ring
OO = O as in phone	

HMONG ALPHABET AND PRONUNCIATIONS

A = ah

B = np = (Ba)

C = Jau

D = Daw

E = A

F = Fa (Fah)

G = G

H = how

I = E

J = J

K = Ko as in cot

L = L

M = M

N = N

O = OU as in off

P = P as in spot

Q = (no english sound)

R = djau

S = S

T = T

U = OO

V = Vā

W = er + w

X = zaw

Y = yaw

Z = zjaw

LINGUISTIC INTERFERENCE WITH
HUNGARIAN/ENGLISH

Sentence Structure: Most of the time, sentence word order is the same as used for English. There are, however, some exceptions.

English:	I see the black dog
Hungarian:	I see the black dog.
English:	The old black dog is running down the road.
Hungarian:	The old black dog is running down the road.

HUNGARIAN ALPHABET	(Eng. pronounciation)	English alphabet	(Hungarian Pronounciation)
A	A (as in Jaw)	A	éj
Á	A (as på)		
B	Bey	B	bi
C	Tsey	C	szi
Cs	Chā		
D	Day	D	di
E	E	E	i
É			
F	Ef	F	ef
G	Gay	G	dzsi
Gy			
H	Ha (as in hah)	H	éjcs
I	Ee (as in feet)	I	áj
Í	Eeee (longer "e")		
J	Ya (as in yes)	J	dzséj
K	Ká (kǎh)	K	kéj
L	El	L	el
M	Em	M	em
N	En	N	en
Ny	Eñya (like Span. tilde)		
O	O (as in go)	O	ou
Ó	Ó (as in go)		
Ö	Ö (like the e of father)		
Ő	O No Eng. equivalent		
P	Pēa	P	pi
no letter Q		Q	kjú
R	Air (trilled R)	R	ár
S	Esh	S	es
Sz	Ess		
T	Tay	T	ti
Ty	Tchǎ		
U	U (as in use)	U	jú
Ú	U (as in use)		

Ü	No Eng. equivalent		
Ü	No Eng. equivalent		
V	Vey	V	vi
no letter W		W	dabolju
X	Iks	X	eksz
Y	Ipsilon	Y	aj
Z	Zay	Z	zi
Zs	Sjay		

Confusing letters or blends: E/i, y/j, w/v, th/d, tr/th, th/s, th/z.

Confusion with the th blend: unvoiced th/tr (tree/three), th/s (thick/sick).

Confusion with the th blend: voiced th/d (the dee, this dis, that dat), th/z (that zat, these zees, this zis).

WORD PAIRS

That/zat
These/zees
This/zis
This/dis
That/dat
They/day
Water/vater
Work/vork
Three/tree
Thick/sick
Trick/sick

LINGUISTIC INTERFERNCE WITH
INDONESIAN/ENGLISH

Syntax Variants

English: The old black dog was running down the road.
Indonesian: Dog black that is old runs the street.
English: I see the black dog.
Indonesian: I see dog black that.

There is only one tense, the present. Ex: Today I cook rice. Yesterday I cook rice.

When speaking, the singular form of the word is said two times. In order to show plural when writing, a small 2 is written:

Anak = (child) singular

Anak^2 = (children) plural

Possessives are indicated by an ending word form (nȳa). The translated possessive is:

English =   The boy's sweater
Indonesian =   Sweater of the boy

There is no form of "to be." I am happy = I happy. Different letter blends or sound transpositions. The unvoiced "th" as in thick = Ti. The voiced th, as in the = da. The final unvoiced th = "T" or F (teet or teef). The letters S/Z are often confused (sipper/zipper) "U/JU", F/V, C=CH. The "C", in Indonesian, has a "CH" sound. Ex: Chair or Children would be spelled (phonetically) cair (no "h") and children (no "h"). The letter "C" never has a "K" sound, always a "CH".

VOWELS

A = ah
E = Āy
I = Ē
O = oh
U = oo as in good
Alphabet sounds are the same as for Dutch with these exceptions:
Q = koo
U = oo as in tooth
G = G as in gay

ALPHABET PRONUNCIATION

A = ah	K = ka	U = oo as in tooth
B = bay	L = L	V = vay
C = say	M = M	W = way
D = day	N = N	X = ix
E = aye	O = O	Y = aie
F = ef	P = pay	Z = zet
G = gay	Q = koo	
H = hah	R = err	
I = e	S = S	
J = yea	T = te	

WORD PAIR COMPARISONS

Sipper	- Zipper
Use	- Juice
Thought	- Taught
Teet	- Teef
Lit	- Lid
Head	- Hat
Whear	- Wear
Then	- Den
Jeep	- Cheep
Jew	- View
Thick	- Tick

LINGUISTIC INTERFERENCE WITH
POLISH/ENGLISH

Syntax Variants

In Polish there are no articles (a, an, the).

Polish distinguishes the formal and informal ways of addressing people. Similarly to Spanish, the pronoun "ty" (you) is used only when addressing close friends, children, etc. "Pan" (masc.) or "pani" (fem.) are used when addressing casual friends, professional or business acquaintances etc. They correspond to the term "usted" in Spanish. The verbs following "pan" or "pani" will then be used in the 3rd person singular rather than in 2nd, which belongs exclusively to the casual "ty".

All nouns, adjectives and verbs in Polish consist of a stem (or root) of the word and a grammatical ending which changes depending on the case in which it appears. All nouns, pronouns and adjectives in Polish have cases and undergo declension. Their "dictionary" form is usually the nominative case. Sometimes, not only the ending of a particular noun, but also the stem itself changes, undergoing some "reshuffling". Therefore, one has to know the nominative case of a given word to be able to locate it in a dictionary. Example:

> To jest <u>pies</u>. This is a <u>dog</u>. (Nominative)
>
> Mam <u>psa</u>. I have a <u>dog</u>. (Accusative).

There are several different declensions in Polish, depending on the gender of nouns or adjectives, as well as their stem endings. Also, in Polish all adjectives have either masculine, feminine or neuter gender, which has to agree with that of the noun they are modifying. <u>Most</u> feminine nouns end in "a", although there are some exceptions. <u>Most</u> masculine nouns end in a consonant.

The function of cases in Polish:

<u>Nominative</u> -	indicates the subject of a sentence
<u>Genitive</u> -	indicates possession (in English replaced by the usage of "of" or "'s"
<u>Dative</u> -	indicates indirect object (in English indicated by the usage of "for" or "to"
<u>Accusative</u> -	indicates direct object (Mam psa. I have a dog)
<u>Instrumental</u> -	indicates by means of instrument: write with a pencil - pisać ołówkiem
<u>Locative</u> -	used after such prepositions as w (in), na (on), o (about) przy (by, near), etc. Indicates placement, location or position.
<u>Vocative</u> -	used when addressing someone directly: Kasiu! Kathy!

A Polish child may, therefore, have difficulty grasping the English syntax where the nouns, pronouns and adjectives do not change their form or endings.

In Polish, the endings of <u>verbs</u> indicate which person they refer to:

I write	-piszę
You write	-piszesz
He, she, it writes	-pisze
etc.	

It is, therefore, not necessary to use pronouns in front of the verbs; their form is self-explanatory. Verbs are conjugated in all three basic tenses (past, present and future). There are also some irregular verbs, whose conjugation does not follow any specific rules.

Simple ("yes or no" type) questions are formed in Polish by adding the word "czy" at the beginning of a simple statement:

> Mam psa. I have a dog.
>
> Czy mam psa? Do I have a dog?

ALPHABET

A - aah

Ą - nasal, does not exist in English

B - bĕh

C - tse

Ć - <u>very</u> soft <u>ch</u>

D - dĕh

E - ĕh

Ę - nasal, similar to "vin" in Fr.

F - e<u>ff</u>

G - geah (as in goat)

H - hah

I - ēē

J - yot

K - kăh

Ł - ell

L - ew (as in <u>water</u>)

M - em

N- en

Ń - soft as in ca<u>ny</u>on

O - o (as in b<u>ought</u>)

Ó - oo (as in p<u>oor</u>)

P - pĕh

Q - koo

R - err (vibrating)

S - ess

Ś - <u>very</u> soft sh

T - tĕh

U - oo (equiv. of O)

W - voo

X - ēēks

Y - egreque

Z - zet

Ż = Ƶ - <u>j</u>et (hard)

Ź - <u>very</u> soft <u>j</u>et

Consonant clusters:

sz - sh

cz - ch

dz - tz - hard for English

rz = z p as in be<u>ige</u>

dź - soft as in <u>j</u>uice, <u>j</u>udge

dż - harder, similar to the above

ch = h = hah

Substitution of hard for soft consonants (sz for s) changes the meaning completely. Example:

> proszę - please (hard sz)
>
> prosię - piglet (soft s)

There is no sound in Polish resembling the English <u>th</u>; therefore children tend to replace it with either "s", "t", or "d".

Word Pairs:

hut - hat	think - sink
blend - bland	thank - sank
slit - sleet	thank - tank
very - vary	thin - tin
green - grin	three - tree

LINGUISTIC INTERFERENCE WITH
PORTUGUESE/ENGLISH

Syntax Variants
English: I see the black dog.
Portuguese: I see the dog black.
The adjective usually comes after the noun.

The second person pronouns "tu" and "vos" are used only in addressing intimate friends, children, etc., and then only in some regions. "Voce" is the more common form for you. When speaking with an older person or one for whom you wish to show respect, "o senhor" and "a senhora" are often used.

GENDER

Masculine, feminine, neuter. Gender is noted by the final letter or letters. English has no gender.

Possessive pronouns and adjectives must agree in gender and number with the nouns to which they refer: My blue books. Meus livors azuis. My blue book. Meu livro azul. Articles must agree in gender and number also.

The date is placed before the name of the month. Ordinal numbers are not used for the date except primeiro. Neither the day of the week nor the month are capitalized: 'Today is thursday, 21 july 1982."

Questions are formed by raising the voice at the end of a statement. The auxiliary verb do is not used.

LETTERS AND SOUNDS

Each vowel is pronounced clearly and crisply.
A single consonant is pronounced with the following vowel.
The tilde (til) (~) over a vowel indicates a nasal sound: Joaõ.

VOWELS

A as in ah, father
E as in eh, best
I as in machine
O as in off and rose
U as in rule

CONSONANTS AND CONSONANT GROUPS

Ch as in machine
H is never pronounced
LH as in million
M an N tend to nasalize the vowel before them, the lips are not closed in pronouncing a
   final M
NH as in onion
S between vowels as Z, or as S in rose; initial S, or SS, as SS in lesson.
C before A, O, and U, and before any other consonant is like C in cat carta-letter

C before E, and I is like the C in center: sincero-sincere (used only before A, O, or D) is like the C in facade: moco-young man.

G before E and I is like the S in measure: gente-people

G otherwise is like g in go: gato-cat

J is similar to g before e and i: jantar-to dine

L is formed with the tongue forward, the tip near the upper teeth: Paleto-jacket

L final L is quite soft: mal-evil

QU before A or O is like QU in quota: quadro-picture

QU before E or I is usually like K: Que?-What?

X has the following sounds: like Z -exame-examination, like SH - caixa-box, like S in see -maximo-maximum, like X in wax: taxi-taxi

VOWEL COMBINATIONS

AI ai as in aisle

AU ou as in out

EI ey as in they

ÉI similar sound with open E

EU ey as in they plus U of lute

ÉU similar but with open E

IA ya as in yard

IÉ ye as in yes

IE similar but with close E

IO yo as in yoke

IU E plus U of lute

OI oy as in boy

ÓI similar but with open O

OU ou as in soul

UA wah, as ua in quadrangle

UÉ we as in wet

UI we (if main stress is on U, however, like U of lute plus E)

UO wo as in woe, or as uo.

NASAL SOUNDS

This nasal quality is especially strong in Brazil; in Continental Portuguese it may be slight or even absent.

M, N and NH, nasal sounds, tend to nasalize the vowel preceding them. M, N followed by a consonant are not pronounced, nor in final position; merely nasalize the preceding vowel.

A, O are nasalized: la-wool, manha-morning.

Nasal vowel combinations: mãe-mother, licões-lessons, mão-hand, põe-he puts.

PUNCTUATION

The dash is used in dialogues to indicate quotations: —Como vai o senhor? Capitals are not used as frequently: eu (I). Decimal points and commas in figures vary: 6.247 metros - 6,247 meters/Cr $4.800,50.

STRESS

Words ending in A, E, or O (or in one of these vowels and S, M, or NS) are stressed on the next to the last syllable: casa - house. Words ending in any letter, in a nasal vowel or diphthong are stressed on the last syllable: papel - paper, descansei - I rested. Words not following the above rules have a written accent mark which indicates the stressed syllable: cafe - coffee.

THE ALPHABET

Letter	Name	Letter	Name
A	a(ah)	N	ene
B	bê	O	ó
C	cê	P	pê (peh)
D	dê	Q	quê (keh)
E	é (eh)	R	erre
F	efe	S	esse
G	gê (jeh)	T	tê
H	agá (ag ah)	U	U (oo)
I	i (e)	V	vê
J	j jota	X	xis (she's)
L	ele	Z	zê
M	eme		

WORD PAIRS

Ship - Sheep
Slip - Sleep
Chip - Cheap
Is - Ease
Will - We'll
Bat - Bet
Pat - Pet
Tin - Teen
Reap - Rip
Feet - Fit

Portuguese speaking students learning English tend to put a vowel on the end of every word ending in a consonant, because most of their words end in vowels. Sometimes a tendency to put a W sound in front of words beginning with a closed vowel is noted.

LINGUISTIC INTERFERENCE WITH
RUSSIAN/ENGLISH

Syntax Variants

The teacher should take into consideration that:

        1). There are no articles (a, an, the) in Russian.

        2). In Russian verb to be in all it's forms of present time is never used, so students may have trouble missing it in English.

English: This is a dog.
Russian: This - - dog.
English: There is a dog.
Russian: There - - dog.

In general, syntax is about the same.

English: There is a black dog.
Russian: There - black - dog.

Sequence of tenses in Russian is not so obligatory as in English. In some combinations of times it's not used at all.

English: I knew that you would come.
Russian   I knew, that you will come.

        3). All animals and other inanimate objects have neuter genders in English. In Russian all objects including inanimate ones are divided into three genders: Masculine, feminine and neuter. For instance the word corresponding to home is masculine, cottage - feminine, building - neuter. The student may use "she" and "he" and their derivatives in a reference to inanimate objects. "He [is a] stone" - speaking about stone. She [is a] cat.

        4). Forms of questioning may be difficult because in Russian it is not necessary to use certain word order. Thus, a question may be stated just by intonation of voice.

English: Will he come?
Russian: He will come?

        5). It also may be helpful to know, that there are six different cases in Russian. This means, that words change their endings in every case similar to Latin.

CONFUSING LETTERS AND SOUND TRANSPOSITIONS

    C = V
    G = D
    E = Yellow
    U = Green
    N = P
    P = sort of R, but harder (rolled)
    C = S, never like K (cat = sat)
    M = T
    Y = Moon, goose
    X = H (hurt)
    R = CH (chair)

SOUNDS

"R" sound must be very difficult. In Russian, it is completely different. It is either rolled or sort of a "growl". Children may pronounce it almost as (Ž) sound (like in confu<u>sio</u>n) or like hard Russian "R" (rolled). Teeth sounds do not exist in Russian. Students may pronounce "th" sound like "f" or "t" or "S" or "Z". "W" sound does not exist, just "V".

In Russian all letters in any word are pronounced. There are no letter combinations. Students may pronounce the last "r" in such words like lette<u>r</u> or may have other difficulties when reading.

Some vowels may be confusing:

B<u>a</u>d - B<u>e</u>d
C<u>o</u>rn - C<u>o</u>n
R<u>ea</u>d - R<u>i</u>d

VOWELS

A = as in f<u>a</u>ther
E = as in y<u>e</u>llow
Ė = as in y<u>o</u>lk
U = as in gr<u>ee</u>n
O = as in c<u>o</u>rn or d<u>og</u>

Y = as in moon
  = as in lid
  = a as in b<u>a</u>d
  = as in c<u>u</u>be
  = as in yard, yarn

WORD PAIRS

Three - free or tree
Think - sink
That - zat
Teeth - teef or tees etc.
Well - vell
Water - vater
Weather - Vezer
Both - Boz

RUSSIAN ALPHABET

Letter	Handwriting	English Equivalent of Pronunciation
А а		hall
Б б		b
В в		v
Г г		g, gun
Д д		d
Е е		yellow
Ё ё		yolk, York
Ж ж		confusion
З з		z
И и		green
Й й		y, toy, joy, clay
К к		k
Л л		l
М м		m
Н н		n
О о		corn, dog
П п		p
Р р		r, (but harder)
С с		s
Т т		t
У у		moon
Ф ф		f
Х х		kh
Ц ц		ts, cats
Ч ч		ch, chair
Ш ш		sh, share
Щ щ		shch, (or a soft sh, fashion)
ь		soft sign, ((мягкий знак))
Ы ы		like oy, boy (only not fully pronouncing the o)
ъ		hard sign, ((твёрдый знак))
Э э		Ed, elephant
Ю ю		cube, cute
Я я		yawn, yard

LINGUISTIC INTERFERENCE WITH
SWEDISH/ENGLISH

Syntax Variants

In Swedish there are some differences in the use and formation of plurals. There are some differences in the use of (ing). The apostrophe is not used in Swedish.

English:	I see the black dog.
Swedish:	I see the black dog.
English:	The old black dog is running down the road.
Swedish:	The old black dog runs down the road.
English:	Let's go to the store.
Swedish:	Now go we to the store.

SOUND TRANSPOSITIONS

V = W, W = V
Very = Wery, Word = Vork
J = Y, Y = U, as in used
Jewel = Yule, J = H as in hide
Z = S
Zoo = Sue

Sometimes the voiced "th" as in the = "da" and the unvoiced "th" as in thin or teeth = "ta". "Ja"/ch.

WORD PAIR COMPARISONS

Yes - Jes　　　　　　Seal- Zeal
Jewel - Yule　　　　Just - Yust
Chest - Jest　　　　Joke - Yoke
Work - Vork　　　　Thank - Tank
Zoo - Sue　　　　　Gin - Chin
Zip - Sip

SWEDISH VOWELS

A = as in father, cut
E = as in elevator, set
I = as in seen, sit
O = as in pool, book
U = yule, flute
Å = raw, caught
Ä = fare, hat
Ö = early, flutter
Y = used, gripped

SWEDISH ALPHABET

A as in father
B as in bed
C as in seance
D as in dentist
E as in elevator
F as in effort
G as in gift
H as in haul
I as in seem
J as in yule, hide
K as in car
L as in long
M as in mother
N as in noise
O as in book

P as in pull
Q as in queen
R as in air
S as in stove
T as in take
U as in view
V as in oven
W (very similar to V)
X as in excellent
Y as in used
Z as in settle
Å as in raw
Ä as in hat
Ö as in early

LINGUISTIC INTERFERENCE WITH
THAI/ENGLISH

Syntax Variants

English:	I see the black dog.
Thai:	I see the dog black.
English:	The old black dog is running down the road.
Thai:	The dog old black is running down the road.

PLURALS

In Thai, plurals are formed by designating the number of objects while using the singular form of the noun. Ex: Seven boys = boy seven, three women = woman, three, etc.

Possessive is shown: I go to my sister's house = I go to the house of my sister. That is my sister's sweater = That is the sweater of my sister.

Tenses are the same as in English.

Word Endings: One of the most difficult problems, when learning English, is getting accustomed to pronouncing the basic endings of words. In English we voice our endings (cake). In Thai, they are not voiced.

Cake will be pronounced cay

Nine will be pronounced nie

Five will be pronounced fie

Went will be pronounced wen, etc.

The use of (ing) is shown by a word form called "Kamlang." It means in the process of. Ex: Running = Kamlang wing (in the process of) run

There are no articles. Instead of articles, classifiers are used. There are approximately 50 of them. Ex: Khon = persons. There are five levels or types of speech—similar to a caste system.

Another problem that a Thai speaker may experience is difficulty pronouncing combined consonants at the beginning of a word.

Ex: Stop will be satop (the 't' is a forced 'd') "sadop"

Space will be space

School will be sagool

Final "L" when preceeded by 'u' or 'a' = N Ex: Beautiful = Beautifoon, Small = smorn, TH = tr (three = tree). Final unvoiced TH = T, with = wit, both = bot. Final "P" as in Stop = 'B', Stob. Sometimes the final 'P' is omitted. Example: Stamp = stam. Other final consonants may be omitted also.

DIFFICULT & CONFUSING LETTERS & COMBINATIONS

		Voiced	Unvoiced (aspirated)
TH	th	The = duh	three = tree
V	V = w	walentine	heawy
CH	ch = sh	(chair)	shair
RL	r = l, l = r	These 2 letters sound the same to the Thai and are difficult to pronounce differently.	
		r a b b i t	labbit
RL	r, l. as endings	(car)	caa
		pail	paero or paeow

T	Our pronounced 't' often sounds to them as a "ch" (their "t" is much clearer) Ex: "ten" almost sounds like "chen"
Endings	Multiple endings like stands, boxes, adapts are very difficult to pronounce.
W	No difference in "w" and "wh", Ex: window & wheel
Z	"Z" may be a bit difficult at first. Zoo = Soo

WORD PAIR COMPARISONS

Fire = Fine, Five	Lie = Light
Hot = Hard	Rice = Lice
Six = Sick	Light = Right
Fry = Fly	Love = Rub
Three = Tree	Free = Flee
Good = Goose	Full = Foon

There are five voice tones. The first is a normal tone and the other four get progressively higher in pitch like in music. Each new tone changes the word meaning.

ALPHABET COMPARISONS

Thai has 44 alphabet characters. These characters can be combined to duplicate English sounds. There are 24 vowels in Thai. Some are written before the consonant, after or above it. The direction of reading and writing is left to right.

SECTION III
Picture Word List of Things (Nouns) from A to Z

Ambulance = _____

Antlers = _____

Arm = _____

Alligator = _____

Apple = _____

Airplane = _____

Ax = _____

Angel = _____

Ant = _____

Anchor = _____

Autoharp = _____   Arrow = _____

Baby = _____

Bubbles = _____

Bobby pin = _____

Butterfly = _____

Bib = _____

Bird = _____

Bed = _____

Bear = _____

Bee = _____

Boat = _____

Bagpipe = _____

Book = _____

Bridge = _____

Boy = _____

Brick = _____

Broom = _____

Ball = _____

Beehive = _____

Barbeque = _____

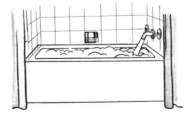

Bathtub = _____

Beaver = _____

Bathrobe = _____

Butcher = _____

Binoculars = _____

Bunkbeds = _____

Boys = _____

Beetle = _____

Bench = _____

Boat = _____

Braids = _____

Bus = _____

Blanket = _____

Brush = _____

Balloon = _____

Bone = _____

Butterchurn = _____

Barn = _____

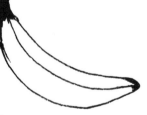

Banana = _____

Bread = _____

Butter = _____

Bat = _____

Boot = _____

Briefcase = _____

Bicycle = _____

Bottle = _____

Block = _____

Birdhouse = _____

Bird = _____

Bell = _____

Badge = _____

Camera = _____

Cow = _____

Cane = _____

Crown = _____

Carrot = _____

Crane = _____

Curtains = _____

Calendar = _____

Crayons = _____

Castle = _____

Cake = _____

Cross = _____

Candle = _____

Celery = _____

Car = _____

Can = _____

Clock = _____

Cat = _____

Corsage = _____

Calf = _____

Crab = _____

Clam = _____

Comb = _____

Crib = _____

Cup = _____

Camel = _____

Cape = _____

Cupid = _____

Cap = _____

Cave = _____

Clothespin = _____

Clown = _____

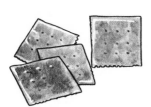

Crackers = _____

Church = _____

Check mark = _____

Cherries = _____

Chain = _____

Chair = _____

Chickens = _____

Chimney = _____

Doorknob = _____

Diving board = _____

Dog = _____

Desk = _____

Drum = _____

Diaper = _____

Dam = _____

Dentist = _____

Dock = _____

Doll = _____

Dinosaur = _____

Donkey = _____

Dice = _____

Doughnut = _____

Dog = _____

Dustpan = _____

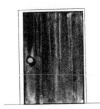

Door = _____

Deer = _____

Duck = _____

Doctor = _____

Drawer = _____

Dragon = _____

Dress = _____

Eleven = _____

Eight = _____

Elevator = _____

Eagle = _____

Envelope = _____

Ear = _____

Egg = _____

Elephant = _____

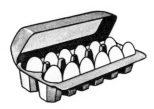

Eggs = _____

Elf = _____

Ferris Wheel = _____

Fairy = _____

Flower = _____

Fly = _____

Five = _____

Furniture = _____

Fireplace = _____

Frog = _____

Fish = _____

Fishbowl = _____

Fruit = _____

Flute = _____

File Cabinet = _____

Flashlight = _____

Fifteen = _____

Flag = _____

Fire = _____

Football = _____

Fire Engine = _____

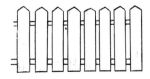

Fence = _____

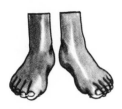

Feet = _____

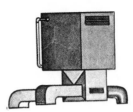

Furnace = _____

Fifty = _____

Four = _____

Feather = _____

Fork = _____

Fox = _____

Fingerprint = _____

Fireworks = _____

Frame = _____

Glove = _____

Girl = _____

Glue = _____

Garbage = _____

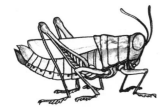

Grasshopper = _____

Glass = _____

Guitar = _____

Gum = _____

Glasses = _____

Gun = _____

Gorilla = _____

Goose = _____

Globe = _____

Grapefruit = _____

Grapes = _____

Graph = _____

Giraffe = _____

Ghost = _____

Garage = _____

Hippopotamus = _____

Hose = _____

Helmet = _____

Hook = _____

Hammer = _____

Hanger = _____

Honey = _____

Handkerchief = _____

Harp = _____

Hand = _____

Handcuffs = _____

Helicopter = _____

Harmonica = _____

Hamburger = _____

Heart = _____

House = _____

Hoe = _____

Horse = _____

Hoof = _____

Horseshoe = _____

Ironing board = _____

Ice skate = _____

Ice cream = _____

Indian chief = _____

Indian squaw = _____

Jacks = _____   Jar = _____

Judge = _____   Jar lid = _____

Jump rope = _____   Jacket = _____

Jail = _____   Jack-in-the-box = _____

Jug = _____   Jeep = _____

Key = _____

Kitten = _____

Kangaroo = _____

Kite = _____

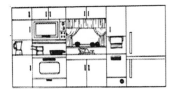

Kitchen = _____

King = _____

Knight = _____

Keyhole = _____

Knife = _____

Knitting needles = _____

Lemon = _____

Log = _____

Lobster = _____

Lantern = _____

Lamb = _____

Leg = _____

Lawnmower = _____

Lady = _____

Lime = _____

Leopard = _____

Lighthouse = _____

Letter = _____

Light switch = _____

Ladder = _____

Lamp = _____

Leaf = _____

Lettuce = _____

Lion = _____

Lightning = _____

Lizard = _____

Lock = _____

Mermaid = _____

Milkman = _____

Mailbox = _____

Marbles = _____

Microphone = _____

Moon = _____

Milk = _____

Mask = _____

Man = _____

Mouse = _____

Microscope = _____

Mop = _____

Map = _____

Matches = _____

Motorcycle = _____

Music = _____

Medal = _____

Mountain = _____

Mailman = _____

Merry-go-round = _____

Measuring spoons = _____   Mouth = _____

Monkey = _____   Mousetrap = _____

Nose = _____

Nurse = _____

Needle = _____

Nest = _____

Note = _____

Nail = _____

Nuts = _____

Nine = _____

Organ =

Orange = _____

Oar = _____

Octopus = _____

Owl = _____

Ostrich = _____

Onion =

One = _____

Pie = _____

Puppet = _____

Paperclip = _____

Pen = _____

Penguin = _____

Pinecone = _____

Pear = _____

Paper (Newspaper) = _____

Piano = _____

Pumpkin = _____

Pirate = _____

Porcupine = _____

Pliers = _____

Popcorn = _____

Pitcher = _____

Paddlewheel boat = _____

Pig = _____

Pinwheel = _____

Parachute = _____

Projector = _____

Pajamas = _____

Piggy bank = _____

Pattern = _____

Purse = _____

Peanut = _____

Peach = _____

Potato = _____

Pillow = _____

Pin = _____

Peacock = _____

Penny = _____

Pocketknife = _____

Pineapple = _____

Pocket = _____

Playpen = _____

Puzzle = _____

Presents = _____

Parrot = _____

Policeofficer = _____

Pencil = _____

Peas = _____

Queen = _____

Rainbow = _____

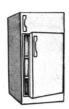

Refrigerator = _____

Rake = _____

Rope = _____

Razor = _____

Rolling pin = _____

Rattle = _____

Ruler = _____

Ring = _____

Raccoon = _____

Rabbit = _____

Rocking chair = _____

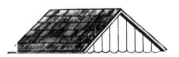

Roof = _____

Rocking horse = _____

Rocket = _____

Rooster = _____

Radio = _____

Saddle = _____

Spoon = _____

Sandle = _____

Safe = _____

Skeleton = _____

Six = _____

Scarf = _____

Skillet = _____

Sled = _____

Stamp = _____

Sun = _____

Spotlight = _____

Swan = _____

Scissors = _____

Swimming pool = _____

Soap = _____

Snail = _____

Scarecrow = _____

Saw = _____

Sailor = _____

Seal = _____

Spool = _____

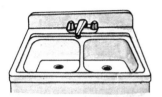

Sink = _____

Sandwich = _____

Sweater = _____

Saltshaker = _____

Skis = _____

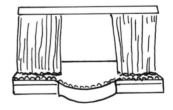

Stage = _____

Star = _____

Stapler = _____

Squirrel = _____

Suitcase = _____

Snowshoe = _____

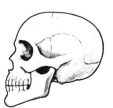

Skull = _____

Soup = _____

Stool = _____

Statue = _____

Slipper = _____

Soldier = _____

Spider = _____

Squash = _____

Snake = _____

Stationwagon car = _____

Stethoscope = _____

Slingshot = _____

Swing = _____

Stagecoach = _____

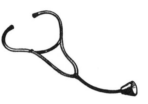

Slide = _____

Spacesuit = _____

Sleigh = _____

Scale = _____

Socks = _____

Sawhorse = _____

Skunk = _____

Submarine = _____

Seven = _____

Spinning wheel = _____

Stove = _____

Soda = _____

Snowman = _____

Strainer = _____

Santa Claus = _____

Sleeve = _____

Swing = _____

Sugar = _____

Shovel = _____

Shirt = _____

Shark = _____

Shelf = _____

Shepherd = _____

Shutters = _____

Shadow = _____

Shower = _____

Shoe = _____

Shell = _____

Ship = _____

Sheep = _____

Truck = _____

Television = _____

Tear = _____

Tennis racket = _____

Tiger = _____

20

Twenty = _____

Tent = _____

Top = _____

Tire = _____

Toothpaste = _____

Ticket = _____

Toothbrush = _____

Telephone booth = _____

Typewriter = _____

Toe = _____

Tie = _____

Turtle = _____

Table = _____

Two = _____

Tweezers = _____

Tornado = _____

Tractor = _____

Ten = _____

Teakettle = _____

Treasure = _____

Tank = _____

Turkey = _____

Tree = _____

Tuba = _____

Tape measure = _____

Telephone = _____

Tooth = _____

Taxi = _____

Toilet = _____

Tomato = _____

Teddy bear = _____

Towel = _____

Tongue = _____

Tube = _____
(Tire innertube)

Triangle = _____

Twelve = _____

Tricycle = _____

Thirteen = _____

Thorn = _____

Thread = _____

Theater = _____

Thumb = _____

Thermos = _____

Thimble = _____

Thermometer = _____

3

Three = _____

Umbrella = _____

Vest = _____

Veil = _____

Valentine = _____

Vegetables = _____

Volcano = _____

Vase = _____

Vacuum sweeper = _____

Violin = _____

Wishbone = _____

Waffle = _____

Woodpecker = _____

Waterfall = _____

Web = _____

Window shade = _____

Wigwam = _____

Witch = _____

Wreathe = _____

Wig = _____

Wagon = _____

Washer = _____

Window = _____

Wallet = _____

Windmill = _____

Wand = _____

Well = _____

Watermelon = _____

Worm = _____

Wolf = _____

Washtub = _____

Walrus = _____

Whistle = _____

Wheel = _____

Wheat = _____

Wheelbarrow = _____

Whip = _____

Whisk broom = _____

Whale = _____

Wheelchair = _____

Xylophone = _____

Yawn = _____

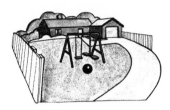

Yard = _____

Yarn = _____

Yo-Yo = _____

Zebra = _____

0

Zero = _____

Zip code = _____

Zipper = _____

Zoo = _____

SECTION IV
Picture Word List of Opposites

Full = _____

Empty = _____

Open = _____

Closed = _____

Day = _____

Night = _____

Push = _____

Pull = _____

Off = _____

On = _____

Awake = _____

Asleep = _____

Cold = _____

Hot = _____

Thin = _____

Fat = _____

Little = _____

Big = _____

Hill = _____

Valley = _____

Up = _____   Down = _____

Young = _____   Old = _____

Under = _____   On = _____

Over = _____   Over = _____

In (inside) = _____   In (inside) = _____

Out = _____

In = _____

Whole = _____

Broken = _____

Short = _____

Long = _____

Far = _____

Close = _____

Small = _____

Big = _____

SECTION V
Picture Word List of Actions

Surprise = _____

Mad = _____

Happy = _____

Sad = _____

Blow bubbles = _____

Run = _____

Chase = _____

Jump = _____

Fight = _____

Lick (Taste) = _____

Planting = _____

Sledding = _____

Sawing = _____

Skating = _____

Buying = _____

Knocking = _____

Making a snowman = _____

Melting = _____

Licking = _____

Feeding = _____

Pulling = _____

Loving = _____

Smelling = _____

Eating = _____

Hanging = _____

Throwing = _____

Blowing bubbles = _____

Digging = _____

Talking = _____

Catching = _____

Kicking = _____

Bouncing a ball = _____

Diving = _____

Batting a ball = _____

Raking leaves = _____

Picking = _____

Painting = _____

Zipping coat = _____

Buttoning coat = _____

Brushing teeth = _____

Washing face = _____   Combing hair = _____

Brushing hair = _____   Tying shoe = _____

Dressing = _____

SECTION VI
Colors, Numbers and Shapes

Teacher,
color me
red.

Teacher,
color me
pink.

Red = _____

Pink = _____

Teacher,
color me
blue.

Teacher,
color me
green.

Blue = _____

Green = _____

Teacher,
color me
orange.

Orange = _____

White = _____

Teacher,
color me
yellow.

Teacher,
color me
brown.

Yellow = _____

Brown = _____

Teacher,
color me
purple.

Teacher,
color me
black.

Purple = _____

Black = _____

1

One = _____

2

Two = _____

3

Three = _____

4

Four = _____

5

Five = _____

6

Six = _____

7

Seven = _____

8

Eight = _____

9

Nine = _____

10

Ten = _____

11

Eleven = _____

16

Sixteen = _____

12

Twelve = _____

17

Seventeen = _____

13

Thirteen = _____

18

Eighteen = _____

14

Fourteen = _____

19

Nineteen = _____

15

Fifteen = _____

20

Twenty = _____

Square = _____   Circle = _____

Triangle = _____   Rectangle = _____

Oval = _____

SECTION VII

The Dolch Word List

This section includes the Dolch Word List* translated into the following langauges:

English (blank)

Croatian	**Indonesian**
Czech	**Polish**
Danish	**Portuguese**
Finnish	**Russian**
Hmong & Mong	**Swedish**
Hungarian	**Thai**

*Reprinted from Edward W. Dolch, *220 Basic Sight Word List,* by permission of the publisher (Copyright, Garrard Publishing Company).

DOLCH BASIC WORD LIST — ENGLISH

Pre-Primer		Primer	
	25. my _____	**Primer**	25. put _____
1. a _____	26. not _____	1. all _____	26. ran _____
2. and _____	27. play _____	2. am _____	27. say _____
3. big _____	28. red _____	3. are _____	28. she _____
4. blue _____	29. ride _____	4. at _____	29. so _____
5. can _____	30. run _____	5. away _____	30. some _____
6. come _____	31. said _____	6. black _____	31. stop _____
7. down _____	32. saw _____	7. but _____	32. thank _____
8. for _____	33. see _____	8. came _____	33. that _____
9. funny _____	34. the _____	9. did _____	34. then _____
10. get _____	35. this _____	10. do _____	35. they _____
11. go _____	36. to _____	11. eat _____	36. three _____
12. green _____	37. up _____	12. fast _____	37. too _____
13. have _____	38. want _____	13. find _____	38. two _____
14. help _____	39. we _____	14. good _____	39. was _____
15. here _____	40. with _____	15. he _____	40. went _____
16. I _____	41. work _____	16. laugh _____	41. what _____
17. in _____	42. you _____	17. like _____	42. where _____
18. is _____		18. new _____	43. white _____
19. it _____		19. no _____	44. will _____
20. jump _____		20. now _____	45. yellow _____
21. little _____		21. on _____	46. yes _____
22. look _____		22. one _____	47. your _____
23. make _____		23. out _____	
24. me _____		24. please _____	

DOLCH BASIC WORD LIST — ENGLISH cont'd.

First		
	21. fly _____	42. may _____	63. us _____
1. about _____	22. found _____	43. much _____	64. very _____
2. after _____	23. four _____	44. must _____	65. walk _____
3. again _____	24. from _____	45. never _____	66. were _____
4. an _____	25. gave _____	46. of _____	67. when _____
5. around _____	26. give _____	47. old _____	68. who _____
6. as _____	27. going _____	48. once _____	69. why _____
7. ask _____	28. had _____	49. open _____	70. wish _____
8. ate _____	29. has _____	50. or _____	
9. be _____	30. her _____	51. our _____	
10. before _____	31. him _____	52. over _____	
11. brown _____	32. his _____	53. pretty _____	
12. by _____	33. how _____	54. round _____	
13. call _____	34. if _____	55. show _____	
14. cold _____	35. into _____	56. sing _____	
15. could _____	36. just _____	57. sleep _____	
16. can't _____	37. know _____	58. soon _____	
17. every _____	38. let _____	59. take _____	
18. far _____	39. long _____	60. them _____	
19. first _____	40. made _____	61. there _____	
20. five _____	41. many _____	62. think _____	

DOLCH BASIC WORD LIST — ENGLISH cont'd.

Second

1. always _____	21. hold _____	42. start _____
2. any _____	22. hot _____	43. tell _____
3. because _____	23. hurt _____	44. ten _____
4. been _____	24. its _____	45. their _____
5. best _____	25. keep _____	46. these _____
6. better _____	26. kind _____	47. those _____
7. both _____	27. light _____	48. today _____
8. bring _____	28. live _____	49. together _____
9. buy _____	29. myself _____	50. try _____
10. carry _____	30. off _____	51. under _____
11. clean _____	31. only _____	52. upon _____
12. cut _____	32. own _____	53. use _____
13. does _____	33. pick _____	54. warm _____
14. done _____	34. pull _____	55. wash _____
15. drink _____	35. read _____	56. well _____
16. fall _____	36. right _____	57. which _____
17. full _____	37. seven _____	58. would _____
18. goes _____	38. shall _____	59. write _____
19. got _____	39. sit _____	60. draw _____
20. grow _____	40. six _____	61. eight _____
	41. small _____	

DOLCH BASIC WORD LIST - CROATIAN

Pre-Primer :

1. a NO ARTICLE	26. not NE	7. but ALI
2. and I	27. play IGRATI (SE)	8. came DOŠAO (JE)
3. big VELIKO	28. red CRVENO	9. did UČINIO (JE)
4. blue PLAVO	29. ride VOZITI (SE)	10. do UČINITI
5. can MOĆI	30. run TRČATI	11. eat JESTI
6. come DOĆI	31. said REKAO (JE)	12. fast BRZO
7. down DOLJE	32. saw VIDIO (JE)	13. find NAĆI
8. for ZA	33. see VIDJETI	14. good DOBRO
9. funny SMIJEŠNO	34. the NO ARTICLE	15. he ON
10. get DOBITI	35. this TO	16. laugh SMIJATI (SE)
11. go IĆI	36. to PREMA	17. like VOLJETI
12. green ZELENO	37. up GORE	18. new NOVO
13. have IMATI	38. want HTJETI	19. no NE
14. help POMOĆI	39. we MI	20. now SADA
15. here OVDJE	40. with SA	21. on NA
16. I JA	41. work RADITI	22. one JEDAN
17. in U	42. you TI (VI, Sie-German) like du &	23. out VAN
18. is JE	**Primer :**	24. please MOLIM
19. it TO	1. all SVE	25. put STAVITI
20. jump SKOČITI	2. am SAM	26. ran TRČATI
21. little MALENO	3. are SMO	27. say REĆI
22. look GLEDATI	4. at KOD	28. she ONA
23. make NAPRAVITI	5. away DALEKO	29. so TAKO
24. please MOLIM	6. black DRNO	30. some NEŠTO
25. my MOJE	7. but ALI	31. stop STATI

DOLCH BASIC WORD LIST - CROATIAN

32. thank __ŽANVALITI (SE)__
33. that __TO__
34. then __ONDA__
35. they __ONI__
36. three __TRI__
37. too __ISTO__
38. two __DVA__
39. was __BIO (JE)__
40. went __IŠAO (JE)__
41. what __ŠTO (ŠTA)__
42. where __GDJE__
43. white __BIJELO__
44. will __ĆE__
45. yellow __ŽUTO__
46. yes __DA__
47. your __TVOJ__

First :

1. about __O__
2. after __IZA, POSLJE__
3. again __OPET__
4. an __NO ARTICLE__
5. around __OKO__
6. as __KAO__
7. ask __PITATI__
8. ate __JEO (JE)__

9. be __BITI__
10. before __PRIJE__
11. brown __SMEDE__
12. by __KOD__
13. call __ZVATI__
14. cold __HLADNO__
15. could __MOGAO (JE)__
16. can't __NE MOŽE__
17. every __SVAKI__
18. far __DALEKO__
19. first __PRVI__
20. five __PET__
21. fly __LETJETI__
22. found __NAŠAO (JE)__
23. four __ČETIRI__
24. from __OD__
25. gave __DAO (JE)__
26. give __DATI__
27. going __IDUĆI__
28. had __IMAO (JE)__
29. has __IMA__
30. her __NJEZINO__
31. him __NJEGA__
32. his __NJEGOVO__
33. how __KAKO__

34. if __AKO__
35. into __U__
36. just __BAŠ__
37. know __ZNATI__
38. let __DATI__
39. long __DUGO__
40. made __NAPRAVIO (JE)__
41. many __MNOGO__
42. may __MOŽE__
43. much __PUNO__
44. must __MORATI__
45. never __NIKAD__
46. of __OD__
47. old __STAR__
48. once __JEDNOM__
49. open __OTVORENO__
50. or __ILI__
51. our __NAŠ__
52. over __PREKO__
53. pretty __LIJEPO__
54. round __OKRUGLO__
55. show __POKAZATI__
56. sing __PJEVATI__
57. sleep __SPAVATI__
58. soon __SKORO__

DOLCH BASIC WORD LIST - CROATIAN

59. take   UZETI

60. them   NJIH

61. there   TAMO

62. think   MISLITI

63. us   NAS

64. very   JAKO

65. walk   IĆI

66. were   GDJE

67. when   KAD

68. who   TKO

69. why   ZAŠTO

70. wish   ŽELJETI

Second :

1. always   UVIJEK

2. any   SVAKI

3. because   JER

4. been   BIO

5. best   NAJBOLJE

6. better   BOLJE

7. both   OBOJE

8. bring   DONIJETI

9. buy   KUPITI

10. carry   NOSITI

11. clean   ČISTO

12. cut   REZATI

13. does

14. done   NAPRAVLJENO

15. drink   PITI

16. fall   PASTI

17. full   PUN

18. goes   IDE

19. got   IMA

20. grow   RASTI

21. hold   DRŽATI

22. hot   VRUCE

23. hurt   BOLITI

24. its   NJEGOVO

25. keep   ČUVATI

26. kind   DOBAR

27. light   SVIJETLO

28. live   ŽIVJETI

29. myself   JA (SAM)

30. off

31. only   SAMO

32. own   IMATI

33. pick   DIĆI

34. pull   VUĆI

35. read   ČITATI

36. right   DESNO

37. seven   SEDAM

38. shall   ĆU

39. sit   SJEDITI

40. six   ŠEST

41. small   MALO

42. start   POČETI

43. tell   REĆI

44. ten   DESET

45. their   NJIHOVO

46. these   OVO

47. those   ONO

48. today   DANAS

49. together   ZAJEDNO

50. try   PROBATI

51. under   ISPOD

52. upon   NA (TO)

53. use   UPOTRIJEBITI

54. warm   TOPLO

55. wash   PRATI

56. well   DOBRO

57. which   KOJE

58. would   BI

59. write   PISATI

60. draw   CRTATI

61. eight   OSAM

DOLCH BASIC WORD LIST - CZECH

PRE-PRIMER

1. a — neurč. člen (jeden)
2. and — a
3. big — veliký
4. blue — modrý
5. can — mohu, dovedu
6. come — přicházím
7. down — dolu, dole
8. for — pro
9. funny — legrační
10. get — dostávám
11. go — jdu
12. green — zelený
13. have — mám
14. help — pomáhám, pomoc
15. here — zde
16. I — já
17. in — v
18. is — je
19. it — to
20. jump — skáču
21. little — malý
22. look — dívám se
23. make — dělám, vyrábím
24. please — prosím
25. my — můj
26. not — ne- (zápor. částice
27. play — hraji, hraji si
28. red — červený
29. ride — jedu
30. run — běžím
31. said — řekl jsem
32. saw — viděl jsem
33. see — vidím
34. the — urč. člen (ten)
35. this — toto
36. to — k (předl s 3.pádem)
37. up — nahoru
38. want — chci
39. we — my
40. with — s
41. work — pracuji
42. you — ty, vy

PRIMER

1. all — všichni, všechno
2. am — jsem
3. are — jsme, jste, jsou
4. at — při, u, ve
5. away — pryč
6. black — černý
7. but — ale
8. came — přišel jsem
9. did — dělal jsem
10. do — dělám
11. eat — jím
12. fast — rychlý, rychle
13. find — nacházím
14. good — dobrý
15. he — on
16. laugh — směji se
17. like — mám rád, jako
18. new — nový
19. no — ne, žádný
20. now — nyní
21. on — na
22. one — jeden
23. out — ven
24. please — prosím

DOLCH BASIC WORD LIST - CZECH

FIRST

25. put	pokládám	
26. ran	běžel jsem	
27. say	říkám	
28. she	ona	
29. so	tak	
30. some	trochu	
31. stop	zastavuji, zastávka	
32. thank	děkuji	
33. that	tamten, že	
34. then	než	
35. they	oni	
36. three	tři	
37. too	také, příliš	
38. two	dva	
39. was	byl, byla, bylo	
40. went	šel jsem	
41. what	co	
42. where	kde, kam	
43. white	bílý	
44. will	budu, chci	
45. yellow	žlutý	
46. yes	ano	
47. your	tvůj, váš	

1. about	kolem, okolo, asi
2. after	po
3. again	opět
4. an	neurč. člen (jeden)
5. around	dokola, okolo
6. as	jak
7. ask	ptám se
8. ate	jedl jsem
9. be	býti
10. before	před (časově)
11. brown	hnědý
12. by	u, vedle
13. call	volám
14. cold	studený, nachlazení
15. could	mohl bych
16. can't	nemohu
17. every	každy
18. far	daleký, daleko
19. first	první
20. five	pět
21. fly	letím, moucha
22. found	našel jsem
23. four	čtyři
24. from	od

25. gave	dal jsem
26. give	dávám
27. going	právě jdu
28. had	měl jsem
29. has	má
30. her	její, ji, ni u
31. him	jemu, mu
32. his	jeho
33. how	jak
34. if	jestliže
35. into	dovnitř
36. just	jenom, právě, přesně
37. know	vím
38. let	nechat
39. long	dlouhý
40. made	udělal jsem, vyrobil
41. many	mnoho
42. may	smím
43. much	hodně
44. must	musím
45. never	nikdy
46. of	(předl s 2. pádem)
47. old	starý
48. once	jednou
49. open	otevírám, otevřený

DOLCH BASIC WORD LIST - CZECH

SECOND

50.	or	nebo		25.	keep	zůstávám, nechávám
51.	our	náš	1.	always	vždy	26. kind — druh, milý
52.	over	přes	2.	any	jakýkoliv	27. light — světlo, světlý
53.	pretty	pěkný, dosti	3.	because	protože	28. live — žiji

50. or — nebo
51. our — náš
52. over — přes
53. pretty — pěkný, dosti
54. round — kulatý
55. show — ukazuji, představení
56. sing — zpívám
57. sleep — spím
58. soon — brzy
59. take — beru
60. them — jim, nich, jim
61. there — tam
62. think — myslím
63. us — náš, nám
64. very — velmi, skutečný
65. walk — prodázím se, procházka
66. were — byli jsme/jste, byli
67. when — kdy, když
68. who — kdo
69. why — proč
70. wish — přeji si, přání

1. always — vždy
2. any — jakýkoliv
3. because — protože
4. been — minulý tvar slovesa "býti"
5. best — nejlepší
6. better — lepší, raději
7. both — oba
8. bring — přináším
9. buy — kupuji
10. carry — nesu
11. clean — čistím, čistý
12. cut — sekám, střih
13. does — dělá
14. done — uděláno
15. drink — piji, nápoj
16. fall — padám, pád, podzim
17. full — plný
18. goes — jde
19. got — dostal jsem
20. grow — rostu, pěstuji
21. hold — držím
22. hot — horký
23. hurt — zranit
24. its — jeho

25. keep — zůstávám, nechávám
26. kind — druh, milý
27. light — světlo, světlý
28. live — žiji
29. myself — já sám
30. off — pryč
31. only — jenom pouze, jediný
32. own — vlastní
33. pick — zvedám, sbírám
34. pull — vytahuji
35. read — čtu, četl jsem
36. right — pravý, správný
37. seven — sedm
38. shall — budu
39. sit — sedím
40. six — šest
41. small — malý
42. start — začínám, začátek
43. tell — říkám
44. ten — deset
45. their — jejich
46. these — tyto, tato
47. those — tamty, tamta
48. today — dnes
49. together — dohromady, spolu

DOLCH BASIC WORD LIST - CZECH

50. try _____ pokouším se, snažím se

51. under _____ pod

52. upon _____ na

53. use _____ užívám

54. warm _____ teplý

55. wash _____ umývám

56. well _____ dobře

57. which _____ který, jenž

58. would _____ bych, byste, by

59. write _____ píši

60. draw _____ kreslím, táhnu

61. eight _____ osm

DOLCH BASIC WORD LIST - DANISH

Pre-Primer

1. a _____ EN
2. and _____ OG
3. big _____ STOR
4. blue _____ BLAA
5. can _____ KAN
6. come _____ KOMME
7. down _____ NED
8. for _____ FOR
9. funny _____ MORSOM
10. get _____ TAGE
11. go _____ GAA
12. green _____ GRØN
13. have _____ HAR
14. help _____ HJELP
15. here _____ HER
16. I _____ JEG
17. in _____ I
18. is _____ ER
19. it _____ DET
20. jump _____ SPRING
21. little _____ LILLE
22. look _____ SE
23. make _____ LAVE
24. me _____ JEG

25. my _____ MIN
26. not _____ IKKE
27. play _____ LEGE
28. red _____ RØD
29. ride _____ RIDE
30. run _____ LØBE
31. said _____ SAGDE
32. saw _____ SAA
33. see _____ SE
34. the _____ DET
35. this _____ DETTE
36. to _____ TIL
37. up _____ OP
38. want _____ ØNSKE
39. we _____ OS
40. with _____ MED
41. work _____ ARBEJDE
42. you _____ DE or DU

Primer

1. all _____ ALLE
2. am _____ ER
3. are _____ ER
4. at _____ PAA or VED
5. away _____ VÆKAE
6. black _____ SORT
7. but _____ MEN
8. came _____ KOM
9. did _____ GJORDE
10. do _____ GØRE
11. eat _____ SPISE
12. fast _____ HURTIGT
13. find _____ FINDE
14. good _____ GOD
15. he _____ HAN
16. laugh _____ LE
17. like _____ LIDE
18. new _____ NY
19. no _____ NEJ
20. now _____ NU
21. on _____ PAA
22. one _____ EN
23. out _____ UD
24. please _____ VÆR SAA VENLIG

25. put _____ LÆG
26. ran _____ LØB
27. say _____ SIGE
28. she _____ HUN
29. so _____ SAA
30. some _____ NOGLE
31. stop _____ STOP
32. thank _____ TAK
33. that _____ DET
34. then _____ SAA
35. they _____ DE
36. three _____ TRE
37. too _____ TIL
38. two _____ TO
39. was _____ VAR
40. went _____ GIK
41. what _____ HVAD
42. where _____ HVOR
43. white _____ HVIDT
44. will _____ VIL
45. yellow _____ GUL
46. yes _____ JA
47. your _____ DIN–DERES

DOLCH BASIC WORD LIST - DANISH

First

1. about CIRCA NÆSTEN
2. after EFTER
3. again IGEN
4. an ET or EN
5. around RUNDTOM
6. as SOM
7. ask SPØRGE
8. ate SPISTE
9. be BLIVE/VÆRE
10. before FØR
11. brown BRUN
12. by VED
13. call KALDE
14. cold KOLD
15. could KUND
16. can't KAN IKKE
17. every ALLE
18. far FJERNT
19. first FØRST
20. five FEM

21. fly FLYVE
22. found FINDE
23. four FIRE
24. from FRA
25. gave GAV
26. give GIVE
27. going GAAR
28. had HAVDE
29. has HAR
30. her HENDE
31. him HAM
32. his HANS
33. how HVORLEDES' HVORDAN
34. if HVIS
35. into INDI
36. just BARE RETFÆROIG
37. know VED
38. let LAD
39. long LANG
40. made LAVET-GJORT
41. many MANGE

42. may MAA
43. much MEGET
44. must SKAL
45. never ALDRIG
46. of AF
47. old GAMMEL
48. once ENGANG
49. open AABEN
50. or ELLER
51. our VORES
52. over OVER
53. pretty PÆN
54. round RUND
55. show FORESTILLING
56. sing SYNGE
57. sleep SOVE
58. soon SNART
59. take TAGE
60. them DEM
61. there DER
62. think TÆNKE

63. us OS
64. very MEGET
65. walk GAA
66. were VAR
67. when HVORNAAR
68. who HVEM
69. why HVORFOR
70. wish ONSKE

DOLCH BASIC WORD LIST - DANISH

Second

1. always ___ALTID___
2. any ___NOGLE___
3. because ___FORDI___
4. been ___VÆRET___
5. best ___BEDSTE___
6. better ___BEDRE___
7. both ___BEGGE___
8. bring ___BRINGE___
9. buy ___KØBE___
10. carry ___BÆRE___
11. clean ___REN___
12. cut ___SNIT___
13. does ___GØR___
14. done ___GJORDT___
15. drink ___TAAR___
16. fall ___FALDE___
17. full ___FULD___
18. goes ___GAAR___
19. got ___HAR–FIK___
20. grow ___VOKSE___

21. hold ___HOLDE___
22. hot ___VARM___
23. hurt ___GØRONDT___
24. its ___DETS DENS___
25. keep ___BEHOLDE___
26. kind ___SLAGS___
27. light ___LYS___
28. live ___LEVENDE___
29. myself ___MIGSELV___
30. off ___AF___
31. only ___KUN___
32. own ___EGEN___
33. pick ___PLUKKE___
34. pull ___TRÆKKE___
35. read ___LÆSE___
36. right ___RIGTIGT___
37. seven ___SYV___
38. shall ___SKAL___
39. sit ___SIDDE___
40. six ___SEKS___
41. small ___LILLE___

42. start ___BEGYNDE___
43. tell ___FORTÆLLE___
44. ten ___TI___
45. their ___DERES___
46. these ___DIS'S'E___
47. those ___DE___
48. today ___I DAG___
49. together ___TILSAMMEN___
50. try ___PRØVE___
51. under ___UNDER___
52. upon ___PAA___
53. use ___BRUGE___
54. warm ___VARM___
55. wash ___VADSKE___
56. well ___GODT___
57. which ___HVILKEN___
58. would ___VILDE___
59. write ___SKRIVE___
60. draw ___TEGNE___
61. eight ___OTTE___

DOLCH BASIC WORD LIST - FINNISH

Pre-Primer :

1.	a	-
2.	and	ja
3.	big	iso, suuri
4.	blue	sininen
5.	can	voida
6.	come	tulla
7.	down	alas, alhaalla
8.	for	-, varten
9.	funny	hassunkurinen
10.	get	saada
11.	go	mennä
12.	green	vihreä
13.	I have	minulla on
14.	help	auttaa; apu
15.	here	tässä, täällä
16.	I	minä
17.	in	-, sisässä, sisällä
18.	is	on
19.	it	se
20.	jump	hypätä
21.	little	pieni
22.	look	katsoa
23.	make	tehdä
24.	please	ole hyvä
25.	my	minun

26.	not	ei
27.	play	leikkiä
28.	red	punainen
29.	ride	ratsastaa, ajaa
30.	run	juosta
31.	said	sanoi
32.	saw	näki
33.	see	nähdä
34.	the	-
35.	this	tämä
36.	to	-, (ending: -lle)
37.	up	ylös, ylhäällä
38.	want	tahtoa, haluta
39.	we	me
40.	with	mukana, kanssa, kera
41.	work	työ; tehdä työtä
42.	you	sinä; te

Primer :

1.	all	kaikki
2.	am	olen
3.	are	olet,olemme,olette, ovat
4.	at	-, luona
5.	away	pois, poissa
6.	black	musta
7.	but	mutta, vaan

7.	but	mutta, vaan
8.	came	tuli
9.	did	teki
10.	do	tehdä
11.	eat	syödä
12.	fast	nopea; nopeasti
13.	find	löytää
14.	good	hyvä
15.	he	hän
16.	laugh	nauraa
17.	like	pitää
18.	new	uusi
19.	no	ei
20.	now	nyt
21.	on	-, päällä
22.	one	yksi
23.	out	ulos, ulkona
24.	please	ole hyvä
25.	put	panna
26.	ran	juoksi
27.	say	sanoa
28.	she	hän
29.	so	niin
30.	some	jotakin, hiukan
31.	stop	pysähtyä

DOLCH BASIC WORD LIST - FINNISH

32.	thank	kiittää; kiitos	9.	be	olla	34.	if	jos
33.	that	että; tuo; joka	10.	before	ennen	35.	into	-
34.	then	sitten	11.	brown	ruskea	36.	just	juuri
35.	they	he	12.	by	-	37.	know	tietää, tuntea
36.	three	kolme	13.	call	soittaa, kutsua	38.	let	antaa, sallia
37.	too	liian; myös	14.	cold	kylmä	39.	long	pitkä
38.	two	kaksi	15.	could	voi, voisi	40.	made	teki
39.	was	oli	16.	can't	ei voi	41.	many	moni, monta
40.	went	meni	17.	every	jokainen	42.	may	voi, saa
41.	what	mikä	18.	far	kauas, kaukana	43.	much	paljon
42.	where	missä	19.	first	ensimmäinen	44.	must	täytyy
43.	white	valkoinen	20.	five	viisi	45.	never	ei koskaan
44.	will	-	21.	fly	lentää	46.	of	-
45.	yellow	keltainen	22.	found	löysi	47.	old	vanha
46.	yes	kyllä	23.	four	neljä	48.	once	kerran
47.	your	sinun; teidän	24.	from	-	49.	open	avata; avoin
First :			25.	gave	antoi	50.	or	tai; eli
1.	about	-	26.	give	antaa	51.	our	meidän
2.	after	jälkeen	27.	going	menossa	52.	over	-, yli
3.	again	jälleen, taas	28.	I had	minulla oli	53.	pretty	kaunis, soma.
4.	an	-	29.	has	hänellä on	54.	round	pyöreä
5.	around	ympäri	30.	her	hänen	55.	show	näyttää
6.	as	kuin, kuten	31.	him	hänelle, häntä	56.	sing	laulaa
7.	ask	kysyä, pyytää	32.	his	hänen	57.	sleep	nukkua
8.	ate	söi	33.	how	kuinka, miten	58.	soon	pian

DOLCH BASIC WORD LIST - FINNISH

59. take	ottaa	13. does	tekee	38. shall	–
60. them	heille, heitä	14. done	tehnyt	39. sit	istua
61. there	siellä, sinne	15. drink	juoda	40. six	kuusi
62. think	ajatella, luulla	16. fall	pudota	41. small	pieni
63. us	meille, meitä	17. full	täysi	42. start	alkaa
64. very	hyvin	18. goes	menee	43. tell	kertoa, käskeä
65. walk	kävellä	19. got	sai	44. ten	kymmenen
66. were	olit, olimme, olitte, olivat	20. grow	kasvaa	45. their	heidän
67. when	kun, koska?	21. hold	pitää	46. these	nämä
68. who	kuka, ketkä	22. hot	kuuma	47. those	nuo
69. why	miksi	23. hurt	satuttaa,koskea	48. today	tänään
70. wish	toivoa,toivottaa	24. its	sen	49. together	yhdessä
Second :		25. keep	pitää	50. try	yrittää
1. always	aina	26. kind	ystävällinen	51. under	alla, alle
2. any	yhtään	27. light	valoisa, kevyt; valo; valaista	52. upon	päällä
3. because	koska	28. live	elää	53. use	käyttää
4. been	ollut	29. myself	itse	54. warm	lämpöinen
5. best	paras	30. off	–	55. wash	pestä
6. better	parempi	31. only	vain; ainoa	56. well	hyvin
7. both	molemmat	32. own	oma	57. which	mikä; joka
8. bring	tuoda	33. pick	poimia, valita	58. would	tahtoisi
9. buy	ostaa	34. pull	vetää	59. write	kirjoittaa
10. carry	kantaa	35. read	lukea	60. draw	piirtää
11. clean	puhdas	36. right	oikea; oikein	61. eight	kahdeksan
12. cut	leikata	37. seven	seitsemän		

DOLCH BASIC WORD LIST - HMONG

PRE-PRIMER

1. a ___ ib(siv tau rau xws li)(ib tug miv) etc.
2. and ___ thiab
3. big ___ loj
4. blue ___ xiav(siv xiav)
5. can ___ muaj cuab kav
6. come ___ los, tuaj
7. down ___ nqis hav
8. for ___ rau,yog
9. funny ___ lom zem
10. get ___ muab
11. go ___ mus
12. green ___ ntsuab (siv ntsuab)
13. have ___ muaj
14. help ___ pab, cawm
15. here ___ qhov nov, ntawm nov
16. I ___ kuv
17. in ___ hauv(nyob hauv)
18. is ___ yog
19. it ___ nws
20. jump ___ caws qia
21. little ___ me ntsis,me
22. look ___ xyuas,saib
23. make ___ ua,tsim
24. please ___ mog, yuad
25. my ___ kuv li
26. not ___ tsi
27. play ___ ua si
28. red ___ liab(siv liab)
29. ride ___ caij(caij nees)
30. run ___ khiav
31. said ___ hais(tag los lawm)
32. saw ___ pom,(tag los)kaw, xyuas, ntsia
33. see ___ xyuas,pom,ntsia
34. the ___
35. this ___ qhov nov
36. to ___ txog
37. up ___ saum,(nyob siab)
38. want ___ xav tau
39. we ___ peb
40. with ___ nrog,uake, sib xws
41. work ___ ua hauj lwm, num
42. you ___ koj

PRIMER

1. all ___ txhia tsav,tag huv tib, si
2. am ___ yog(siv rau kuv)
3. are ___ yog(koj yog, nej yog)
4. at ___ qhov ntawd
5. away ___ tawm mus, txav deb
6. black ___ dub(siv dub)
7. but ___ tiam sis
8. came ___ los, tuaj (tag los)
9. did ___ ua(tag los lawm)
10. do ___ ua
11. eat ___ noj
12. fast ___ ceev,nrawm,sai
13. find ___ pom, ntsib
14. good ___ zoo
15. he ___ nws(txiv neej)
16. laugh ___ luag
17. like ___ nyiam,ib yam, sibluag
18. new ___ tshiab
19. no ___ tsi, (tsi tau)
20. now ___ tam sim no
21. on ___ saum
22. one ___ ib
23. out ___ tawm,rho, nraum
24. please ___ mog,yuad

DOLCH BASIC WORD LIST - HMONG

FIRST

25. put _____ ntsaws rau

26. ran _____ qhiav(tag los)

27. say _____ hais

28. she _____ nws (poj niam)

29. so _____ ib yam (ib yam li)

30. some _____ me ntsis

31. stop _____ nres

32. thank _____ ua tsaug

33. that _____ tom,ntawd

34. then _____ tom qab ntawd

35. they _____ lawv

36. three _____ peb

37. too _____ ib yam, sib npaug

38. two _____ ob

39. was _____ yog(tag los)

40. went _____ mus(tag los)

41. what _____ dab tsi

42. where _____ qhov twg

43. white _____ dawb

44. will _____ yuav(tom ntej)

45. yellow _____ daj

46. yes _____ wj,yog,awj

47. your _____ koj li

1. about _____ ntshig txog kwv yees

2. after _____ tom qab ntawd

3. again _____ dua thiab

4. an _____ ib qhov(siv rau tsav xwb)

5. around _____ ncig

6. as _____ xws li

7. ask _____ nug,thom

8. ate _____ noj(tag los)

9. be _____ yog

10. before _____ ua ntej

11. brown _____

12. by _____ nrog,uake,dhau

13. call _____ hu

14. cold _____ no

15. could _____ muaj cuab kav

16. can't _____ tsi muaj cuab kay

17. every _____ txhia txhia (tsav)

18. far _____ deb deb

19. first _____

20. five _____ tsib

21. fly _____ ya

22. found _____ ntsib,pom,tau

23. four _____ plaub

24. from _____ los,tuaj,ncaim

25. gave _____ muab(tag los)

26. give _____ muab

27. going _____ mus(tab tom)

28. had _____ muaj(tag los)

29. has _____ muaj(nws muaj)

30. her _____ nws(poj niam)

31. him _____ nws(txiv neej)

32. his _____ nws li(txivneej)

33. how _____ yuav ua li cas

34. if _____ yog tias

35. into _____ hauv,ncaj nraim mus

36. just _____ nyuam qhuav

37. know _____ paub

38. let _____ kom

39. long _____ ntev,qeeb

40. made _____ ua(tag los)

41. many _____ ntau ntau

42. may _____ tej zaum

43. much _____ ntau(siv rau tsav suav tsitau

44. must _____ yuav tsum

45. never _____ tsi txeev

46. of _____ yog,uas yog

47. old _____ lau

48. once _____ ib zaug

49. open _____ qhib

DOLCH BASIC WORD LIST - HMONG

SECOND

50. or _____ los yog
51. our _____ peb li
52. over _____ dhau lawm,hla
53. pretty _____ zoo,zoo nkauj
54. round _____ ncig
55. show _____ qhia,yam
56. sing _____ hu nkauj
57. sleep _____ tsaug zog
58. soon _____ tsi ntev, ti ti (tsi ntev saum ntej no)
59. take _____ muab,Nqa
60. them _____ lawv
61. there _____ tom
62. think _____ xav
63. us _____ peb
64. very _____ ntau
65. walk _____ muskev
66. were _____ yog(tag los)
67. when _____ thaum twg
68. who _____ leej twg
69. why _____ vim li ca
70. wish _____ xav tau

1. always _____ tib yam,sib laug
2. any _____ tej tsav
3. because _____ rau qhov
4. been _____ yog(tag los)
5. best _____ zoo kawg
6. better _____ zoo dua
7. both _____ ob tug, obtsav, nkawm
8. bring _____ coj,nqa
9. buy _____ yuav
10. carry _____ nqa,puag,tuav
11. clean _____ so,txhuam,cheb
12. cut _____ txiav,ntov
13. does _____ ua
14. done _____ tiav,tag lawm
15. drink _____ hau
16. fall _____ vau,poob,ntog
17. full _____ puv,pov
18. goes _____ mus, twb
19. got _____ tau lawm, twb muab lawm
20. grow _____ loj hlob
21. hold _____ tuav,coj,nqa npaj,txheem
22. hot _____ kuv,ceev
23. hurt _____ mob
24. its _____ nws li

25. keep _____ ceev cia, khaws cia, tuav cia
26. kind _____ tsav
27. light _____ teeb,pom kev
28. live _____ nyob
29. myself _____ kuv tus kheej
30. off _____ tag,tawm
31. only _____ xwb
32. own _____ tuo kheej tus tswv kheej
33. pick _____ de,lov
34. pull _____ ngus,rub
35. read _____ twm,nyeem
36. right _____ raug,sab xis yog
37. seven _____ xya
38. shall _____ yuav
39. sit _____ zaum,nyob
40. six _____ rau
41. small _____ me
42. start _____ chiv,pib,cuab
43. tell _____ ghia
44. ten _____ kaum
45. their _____ lawv li
46. these _____ tsav no
47. those _____ tsav ntawd
48. today _____ hnub no
49. together _____ uake

DOLCH BASIC WORD LIST - HMONG

50. try _____ sim,xyuam _____

51. under _____ hauv gab _____

52. upon _____ saum,pem _____

53. use _____ siv _____

54. warm _____ sov _____

55. wash _____ ntxuav _____

56. well _____ zoo, yog _____

57. which _____ xws li _____

58. would _____ yuav _____

59. write _____ sau(sau ntawv)

60. draw _____ zo duab _____

61. eight _____ yim _____

DOLCH BASIC WORD LIST - MONG BLUE

PRE-PRIMER

1.	a	
2.	and	thab
3.	big	luj
4.	blue	xav (siv xav)
5.	can	muaj cuab kaav
6.	come	tuaj,lug
7.	down	nqeg haav, nqeg taug
8.	for	yog rua
9.	funny	lom zem
10.	get	muab,tau
11.	go	moog
12.	green	ntsuab
13.	have	muaj
14.	help	paab, cawm
15.	here	nuav,ghov nuav
16.	I	kuv
17.	in	huv
18.	is	yog
19.	it	nwg(siv rua tsaj)
20.	jump	caws qa txoom pwm
21.	little	miv ntsiv
22.	look	saib
23.	make	ua
24.	please	mog,yuad

25.	my	kuv le
26.	not	tsi(tsi yog)
27.	play	Ua si
28.	red	lab(siv lab)
29.	ride	caij(caij neeg)
30.	run	dla
31.	said	has (tau has)
32.	saw	kaw,pum lawm
33.	see	pum
34.	the	
35.	this	nuav,qhov nuav
36.	to	txug
37.	up	sau (nyob sab)
38.	want	xaavtau
39.	we	peb
40.	with	nrug,sib xws, ua ke
41.	work	num, ua num
42.	you	koj

PRIMER

1.	all	txhua tsaav taag,huv tuab si
2.	am	yog(siv rua kuv)
3.	are	yog(siv rua koj)
4.	at	qhov(qhov ntawd)
5.	away	txaav dleb
6.	black	dlub
7.	but	tuam sis
8.	came	Lug;tuaj (tag lug lawm)
9.	did	Ua (tag lug lawm lawm)
10.	do	Ua(au dlej num)
11.	eat	Noj
12.	fast	Ceev,nrawm,sai
13.	find	Ntsib,pom,tau
14.	good	zoo
15.	he	nwg(qua yawg)
16.	laugh	luag
17.	like	nyam,sib xws, sib luag
18.	new	tshab
19.	no	tsi
20.	now	tam sim nua
21.	on	sau
22.	one	Ib
23.	out	tawm,rhu,nrau
24.	please	mog,yuad

DOLCH BASIC WORD LIST - MONG BLUE

FIRST

25. put _____ ntsaws rua	1. about _____ kwv yees, ntshig txug	25. gave _____ muab(taag lug)
26. ran _____ dla(taag lug)	2. after _____ tom qaab	26. give _____ muab
27. say _____ has	3. again _____ dlua thab	27. going _____ moog(taag tom)
28. she _____ nwg(qua puj)	4. an _____	28. had _____ muaj(taag lug)
29. so _____ Ib yaam le	5. around _____ ncig	29. has _____ muaj(nwg muaj)
30. some _____ miv ntsiv, qee tsaav	6. as _____ xws le	30. her _____ nwg(quaspuj)
31. stop _____ nreg	7. ask _____ nug,thom	31. him _____ nwg(quas yawg)
32. thank _____ ua tsaug	8. ate _____ noj(taag lug)	32. his _____ nwgle(quas yawg) yuav ua le caag
33. that _____ ntawd,tod	9. be _____ yog	33. how _____
34. then _____ tom qaab ntawd	10. before _____ ua ntej	34. if _____ yog tas
35. they _____ puab	11. brown _____	35. into _____ huv, ncaaj nraim
36. three _____ peb	12. by _____ nrug, dhlau, ua ke	36. just _____ nyav qhuav(nyav qhuav,moog,kag)
37. too _____ tuab yaam, sib npaug	13. call _____ hu	37. know _____ paub
38. two _____ ob	14. cold _____ no, txag	38. let _____ kua(kua nwg moog)
39. was _____ yog(taag lug)	15. could _____ muaj cuab kaav	39. long _____ ntev
40. went _____ moog(taag lug)	16. can't _____ tsi muaj cuab kaav	40. made _____ ua (taag lug)
41. what _____ dlaab tsi	17. every _____ txhua txhua (tssav)	41. many _____ ntau ntau
42. where _____ qhov twg	18. far _____ dleb	42. may _____ tej zag
43. white _____ dlawb	19. first _____	43. much _____ ntau(siv rua, tsaav suav tsitau)
44. will _____ yuav(tom ntej)	20. five _____ tsib	44. must _____ yuav tsum
45. yellow _____ dlaaj	21. fly _____ yaa	45. never _____ tsi txeev
46. yes _____ yog,awj,wj	22. found _____ ntsib,pum,tau	46. of _____ yog,kws yog
47. your _____ koj le	23. four _____ plaug	47. old _____ laug
	24. from _____ ncaim, tuaj lug	48. once _____ ib zag
		49. open _____ qheb

DOLCH BASIC WORD LIST - MONG BLUE

SECOND

50. or	los yog	25. keep	khaws, ceev, tuav
51. our	peb le	26. kind	tsaav
52. over	dhlau lawm, hlaa	27. light	teeb,pum kev
53. pretty	zoo,zoo nkauj	28. live	nyob
54. round	ncig	29. myself	kuv tug kheej
55. show	qha,yaam	30. off	taag,tawm
56. sing	hu nkauj	31. only	xwb,tuab qhov
57. sleep	tsaug zug	32. own	tug kheej le
58. soon	tsi ntev,ti ti (tsi ntev sau ntej nuav)	33. pick	dle,luv
59. take	muab,nqaa	34. pull	nqug
60. them	puab	35. read	nyeem(nyeem ntawv)
61. there	tom,tod	36. right	raug,yog, saab xis
62. think	xaav	37. seven	xyaa
63. us	peb	38. shall	yuav (yuav moog)
64. very	ntau	39. sit	nyob tsawg
65. walk	moog kev,moog	40. six	rau
66. were	yog (taag lug lawm)	41. small	miv,miv quav
67. when	thaum twg	42. start	cuab,chiv,pib
68. who	leej twg	43. tell	gha
69. why	vim le caag	44. ten	kaum
70. wish	xaav tau	45. their	puab le

1. always	tuab yaam, sib kws, sib luag
2. any	tej tsaav
3. because	rau qhov
4. been	yog, (tub yog taag lug lawm)
5. best	zoo tshaaj plawg
6. better	zoo tshaaj
7. both	nkawm,ob tug ob tsaav
8. bring	coj,nqaa
9. buy	yuav(yuav them nyaj)
10. carry	nqaa,puag, tuav coj
11. clean	txhuam,so,cheb
12. cut	txav,ntuv
13. does	ua
14. done	tav,taag, ua taag lawm
15. drink	hau(hau dlej)
16. fall	qaug,poob,dlog
17. full	puv
18. goes	moog(siv rua nwg)
19. got	tau,tub tau lawm
20. grow	luj, hlub
21. hold	tuav,nqaa,coj npaaj,txheem
22. hot	kub,ceev
23. hurt	mob
24. its	nwg le(siv rua tsa hab tsaav tshaj xwm)

46. these	tsaav nuav
47. those	tsaav ntawd
48. today	nub nua,(nuav)
49. together	ua ke

DOLCH BASIC WORD LIST - MONG BLUE

50. try _____ xyuam,sim _____

51. under _____ huv qaab _____

52. upon _____ saum,peg _____

53. use _____ siv _____

54. warm _____ suv _____

55. wash _____ xtxuav _____

56. well _____ zoo,yog _____

57. which _____ xws le _____

58. would _____ yuav(yuav ua) _____

59. write _____ sau _____

60. draw _____ zo dluab _____

61. eight _____ yim _____

DOLCH BASIC WORD LIST - HUNGARIAN

PRE-PRIMER

1. a _____ egy
2. and _____ és
3. big _____ nagy
4. blue _____ kék
5. can _____ tud
6. come _____ jön
7. down _____ le
8. for _____ miatt
9. funny _____ vicces
10. get _____ kap
11. go _____ megy
12. green _____ zöld
13. have _____ vknek,vmijevan
14. help _____ segít
15. here _____ itt
16. I _____ én
17. in _____ be
18. is _____ van
19. it _____ az,azt
20. jump _____ ugrik
21. little _____ kevés
22. look _____ néz
23. make _____ csinál
24. me _____ engem
25. my _____ enyém
26. not _____ nem
27. play _____ játszik
28. red _____ piros
29. ride _____ lovagol
30. run _____ szalad
31. said _____ mondta
32. saw _____ látta
33. see _____ lát
34. the _____ a
35. this _____ ez
36. to _____ -hoz, -hez
37. up _____ föl
38. want _____ akar
39. we _____ mi
40. with _____ -val, -vel
41. work _____ dolgozik
42. you _____ te, ti

PRIMER

1. all _____ mind
2. am _____ vagyok
3. are _____ vagy
4. at _____ -nál,-nél
5. away _____ távolban
6. black _____ fekete
7. but _____ de
8. came _____ jött
9. did _____ tett
10. do _____ tesz
11. eat _____ eszik
12. fast _____ gyors
13. find _____ talál
14. good _____ jó
15. he _____ ö
16. laugh _____ nevet
17. like _____ szeret
18. new _____ új
19. no _____ nem,ne
20. now _____ most
21. on _____ rajta
22. one _____ egy
23. out _____ ki, kinn
24. please _____ kérem

DOLCH BASIC WORD LIST - HUNGARIAN

FIRST

25. put _____ tesz _____

26. ran _____ futott _____

27. say _____ mond _____

28. she _____ ö _____

29. so _____ úgy _____

30. some _____ néhány _____

31. stop _____ megáll _____

32. thank _____ köszönöm _____

33. that _____ az _____

34. then _____ akkor _____

35. they _____ ök _____

36. three _____ három _____

37. too _____ is, szintén _____

38. two _____ kettö _____

39. was _____ volt _____

40. went _____ ment _____

41. what _____ mi,mit _____

42. where _____ hol _____

43. white _____ fehér _____

44. will _____ fog _____

45. yellow _____ sárga _____

46. yes _____ igen _____

47. your _____ tied _____

1. about _____ körül _____

2. after _____ után _____

3. again _____ újra _____

4. an _____ egy _____

5. around _____ körbe _____

6. as _____ mint _____

7. ask _____ kérdez _____

8. ate _____ evett _____

9. be _____ lenni _____

10. before _____ elött _____

11. brown _____ barna _____

12. by _____ mellett _____

13. call _____ hiv _____

14. cold _____ hideg _____

15. could _____ tudott _____

16. can't _____ nem tud _____

17. every _____ minden _____

18. far _____ messze _____

19. first _____ elsö _____

20. five _____ öt _____

21. fly _____ repül _____

22. found _____ talált _____

23. four _____ négy _____

24. from _____ honnan _____

25. gave _____ adott _____

26. give _____ ad _____

27. going _____ megy _____

28. had _____ vknek vmije volt _____

29. has _____ neki van _____

30. her _____ az ö _____

31. him _____ öt _____

32. his _____ az ö _____

33. how _____ hogyan _____

34. if _____ ha _____

35. into _____ bele _____

36. just _____ éppen _____

37. know _____ tud _____

38. let _____ enged _____

39. long _____ hosszu _____

40. made _____ csinált _____

41. many _____ sok _____

42. may _____ szabad _____

43. much _____ sok _____

44. must _____ kell _____

45. never _____ soha _____

46. of _____ -ból,-tól _____

47. old _____ öreg _____

48. once _____ egyszer _____

49. open _____ nyilt _____

DOLCH BASIC WORD LIST - HUNGARIAN

SECOND

50. or	vagy	1. always	mindig
51. our	miénk	2. any	bármely
52. over	fölött	3. because	mert
53. pretty	csinos	4. been	volt
54. round	kerek	5. best	legjobb
55. show	mutat	6. better	jobb
56. sing	énekel	7. both	mindket
57. sleep	alszik	8. bring	hoz
58. soon	nemsokára	9. buy	vásárol
59. take	vesz	10. carry	visz
60. them	öket	11. clean	tiszta
61. there	ott	12. cut	vág
62. think	gondol	13. does	tesz
63. us	minket	14. done	készített
64. very	nagyon	15. drink	iszik
65. walk	sétal	16. fall	esik
66. were	voltak	17. full	tele
67. when	mikor	18. goes	megy
68. who	ki	19. got	kapott
69. why	miért	20. grow	fejlödik
70. wish	kiván	21. hold	tart
		22. hot	forró
		23. hurt	fáj
		24. its	övé

25. keep	tart
26. kind	kedves
27. light	könnyü
28. live	el
29. myself	magam
30. off	mellette
31. only	csak
32. own	saját
33. pick	felvesz
34. pull	húz
35. read	olvas
36. right	jobbra
37. seven	hét
38. shall	fog
39. sit	ül
40. six	hat
41. small	kicsi
42. start	kezd
43. tell	mond
44. ten	tiz
45. their	as ö
46. these	ezek
47. those	azok
48. today	máma
49. together	együtt

DOLCH BASIC WORD LIST - HUNGARIAN

50. try _____ próbál _____

51. under _____ alatt _____

52. upon _____ rajta _____

53. use _____ használ _____

54. warm _____ meleg _____

55. wash _____ mos _____

56. well _____ jól _____

57. which _____ melyik _____

58. would _____ volna _____

59. write _____ ir _____

60. draw _____ rajzol _____

61. eight _____ nyolc _____

DOLCH BASIC WORD LIST - INDONESIAN

PRE-PRIMER

1. a _____
2. and _____ dan - serta
3. big _____ besar
4. blue _____ biru
5. can _____ dapat bisa
6. come _____ datang
7. down _____ bawah
8. for _____ untuk bagi
9. funny _____ lucu
10. get _____ menerima
11. go _____ pergi
12. green _____ hijau
13. have _____ mempunyai - punya
14. help _____ tolong
15. here _____ disini
16. I _____ saya - aku
17. in _____ didalam
18. is _____ adalah
19. it _____ itu
20. jump _____ meloncat
21. little _____ kecil
22. look _____ melihat
23. make _____ membuat
24. please _____ marie - tolong

25. my _____ saya punya
26. not _____ tidak - bukan
27. play _____ bermain
28. red _____ merah
29. ride _____ naik
30. run _____ lari
31. said _____ berkata
32. saw _____ melihat
33. see _____ melihat
34. the _____ itu
35. this _____ ini
36. to _____ ke
37. up _____ naik
38. want _____ mau
39. we _____ kita - kami bersama
40. with _____ dengan
41. work _____ bekerja
42. you _____ kamu - anda

PRIMER

1. all _____ semua
2. am _____
3. are _____
4. at _____ ke - di
5. away _____ pergi
6. black _____ hitam
7. but _____ tetapi
8. came _____ datang
9. did _____
10. do _____
11. eat _____ makan
12. fast _____ cepat
13. find _____ mendapat
14. good _____ baik
15. he _____ dia - ia
16. laugh _____ ketawa
17. like _____ suka
18. new _____ baru
19. no _____ tidak - bukan
20. now _____ sekarang
21. on _____ di atas
22. one _____ satu
23. out _____ luar
24. please _____

DOLCH BASIC WORD LIST - INDONESIAN

FIRST

25. put _meletakkan_	1. about _tentang_	25. gave _beri_
26. ran _lari_	2. after _sesudah_	26. give _beri_
27. say _berkata_	3. again _lagi_	27. going _pergi_
28. she _dia - ia_	4. an _____	28. had _mempunyai_
29. so _jadi_	5. around _sekeliling_	29. has _mempunyai_
30. some _berberapa_	6. as _seperti_	30. her _dia punya_
31. stop _berenti_	7. ask _bertanyak_	31. him _dia_
32. thank _terima kasih_	8. ate _makan_	32. his _dia punya_
33. that _itu_	9. be _____	33. how _bagaimana_
34. then _pada waktu itu_	10. before _sebelumnya_	34. if _jikalau_
35. they _mereka_	11. brown _coklat_	35. into _kedalam_
36. three _tiga_	12. by _oleh_	36. just _saja - cuma_
37. too _juga_	13. call _memanggil_	37. know _tahu - mengetahui_
38. two _dua_	14. cold _dingin_	38. let _biarlah_
39. was _____	15. could _bisa - dapat_	39. long _panjang - lama_
40. went _pergi_	16. can't _tidak bisa_	40. made _dibuat_
41. what _apa_	17. every _setiap_	41. many _banyak_
42. where _dimana_	18. far _jauh_	42. may _boleh_
43. white _putih_	19. first _pertama_	43. much _banyak_
44. will _akan_	20. five _lima_	44. must _harus_
45. yellow _kuning_	21. fly _terbang_	45. never _tidak pernah_
46. yes _ya_	22. found _mendapat_	46. of _dari punya_
47. your _kamu punya_	23. four _empat_	47. old _tua_
	24. from _dari_	48. once _sekali_
		49. open _buka - terbuka_

DOLCH BASIC WORD LIST - INDONESIAN

SECOND

50. or — atau	1. always — selalu	25. keep — memegang
51. our — kita punya	2. any — siapa-pun	26. kind — macam
52. over — atas	3. because — karena	27. light — terang
53. pretty — indah	4. been —	28. live — hidup
54. round — bulat - bundar	5. best — terbaik	29. myself — saya sendiri
55. show — melihatkan	6. better — lebih baik	30. off —
56. sing — menyanyi	7. both — keduanya	31. only — hanya - saja
57. sleep — tidur	8. bring — membawah	32. own — diri-sendiri
58. soon — cepat	9. buy — membeli	33. pick — memetik
59. take — mengambil	10. carry — membawah	34. pull — menarik
60. them — mereka	11. clean — bersih - membersihkan	35. read — membaca
61. there — disana	12. cut — potong	36. right — benar (kanan) (correct)(direction)
62. think — memikir(kan)	13. does —	37. seven — tujuh
63. us — kita	14. done — sudah selesai	38. shall — akan
64. very — sangat - sekali	15. drink — minum	39. sit — duduk
65. walk — barjalan	16. fall — jatuh	40. six — enam
66. were — dimana	17. full — penuh	41. small — kecil
67. when — kapan	18. goes — pergi	42. start — mulai
68. who — siapa	19. got — dapat	43. tell — mengata-ngatai
69. why — mengapa	20. grow — timbul - tumbuh	44. ten — sepuluh
70. wish — ingin	21. hold — memegang	45. their — mereka punya
	22. hot — panas	46. these — ini
	23. hurt — sakit	47. those — itu
	24. its — kepunyaanya	48. today — hari ini
		49. together — bersama-sama

DOLCH BASIC WORD LIST - INDONESIAN

50. try _____ mencoba _____

51. under _____ dibawah _____

52. upon _____ diatas _____

53. use _____ memakai _____

54. warm _____ panas _____

55. wash _____ mencuci _____

56. well _____ baik _____

57. which _____ yang mana _____

58. would _____ akan _____

59. write _____ menulis _____

60. draw _____ menggambar _____

61. eight _____ delapan _____

DOLCH BASIC WORD LIST - POLISH

PRE-PRIMER

1. a _____ does not exist
2. and _____ i
3. big _____ duży
4. blue _____ niebieski
5. can _____ móc
6. come _____ przyjść
7. down _____ na dole
8. for _____ dla
9. funny _____ śmieszny
10. get _____ dostać
11. go _____ iść
12. green _____ zielony
13. have _____ mieć
14. help _____ pomoc
15. here _____ tutaj
16. I _____ ja
17. in _____ w
18. is _____ jest
19. it _____ to
20. jump _____ skakać
21. little _____ mały
22. look _____ patrzeć
23. make _____ robić
24. please _____ proszę

25. my _____ mój
26. not _____ nie
27. play _____ bawić się
28. red _____ czerwony
29. ride _____ jechać
30. run _____ biec
31. said _____ powiedział
32. saw _____ zobaczył
33. see _____ widzieć
34. the _____ does not exist
35. this _____ ten
36. to _____ do
37. up _____ w górę
38. want _____ chcieć
39. we _____ my
40. with _____ z
41. work _____ pracować
42. you _____ ty

PRIMER

1. all _____ wszyscy
2. am _____ jestem
3. are _____ są
4. at _____ w
5. away _____ does not exist
6. black _____ czarny
7. but _____ ale
8. came _____ przyszedł
9. did _____ zrobił
10. do _____ robić
11. eat _____ jeść
12. fast _____ szybko
13. find _____ znaleźć
14. good _____ dobry
15. he _____ on
16. laugh _____ smiać się
17. like _____ lubić
18. new _____ nowy
19. no _____ nie
20. now _____ teraz
21. on _____ na
22. one _____ jeden
23. out _____ poza
24. please _____ proszę

DOLCH BASIC WORD LIST - POLISH

FIRST

25. put _____ położyć
26. ran _____ biegł
27. say _____ mówić
28. she _____ ona
29. so _____ więc
30. some _____ niektóre
31. stop _____ przestać
32. thank _____ dziękować
33. that _____ tamten
34. then _____ potem
35. they _____ oni
36. three _____ trzy
37. too _____ także
38. two _____ dwa
39. was _____ był
40. went _____ poszedł
41. what _____ co
42. where _____ gdzie
43. white _____ biały
44. will _____ będzie
45. yellow _____ żółty
46. yes _____ tak
47. your _____ twój

1. about _____ o
2. after _____ po
3. again _____ znowu
4. an _____ nonexistent
5. around _____ dokoła
6. as _____ jak
7. ask _____ pytać
8. ate _____ zjadł
9. be _____ być
10. before _____ przed
11. brown _____ brązowy
12. by _____ przy
13. call _____ wołać
14. cold _____ zimny
15. could _____ mógł
16. can't _____ nie nóc
17. every _____ każdy
18. far _____ daleko
19. first _____ pierwszy
20. five _____ pięć
21. fly _____ latać
22. found _____ znalazł
23. four _____ cztery
24. from _____ od

25. gave _____ dał
26. give _____ dać
27. going _____ idący
28. had _____ miał
29. has _____ ma
30. her _____ jej
31. him _____ nim
32. his _____ jego
33. how _____ jak
34. if _____ jeżeli
35. into _____ do, w
36. just _____ tylko
37. know _____ wiedzieć
38. let _____ pozwolić
39. long _____ długi
40. made _____ zrobiony
41. many _____ dużo
42. may _____ moze
43. much _____ wiele
44. must _____ musi
45. never _____ nigdy
46. of _____ nonexistent by itself
47. old _____ stary
48. once _____ raz
49. open _____ otwierać

DOLCH BASIC WORD LIST - POLISH

SECOND

50. or _____ albo _____
51. our _____ nasz _____
52. over _____ nad _____
53. pretty _____ ładny _____
54. round _____ okrągły _____
55. show _____ pokazać _____
56. sing _____ śpiewać _____
57. sleep _____ spać _____
58. soon _____ wkrótce _____
59. take _____ brać _____
60. them _____ ich _____
61. there _____ tam _____
62. think _____ myśleć _____
63. us _____ nas _____
64. very _____ bardzo _____
65. walk _____ chodzić _____
66. were _____ byli _____
67. when _____ kiedy _____
68. who _____ kto _____
69. why _____ dlaczego _____
70. wish _____ pragnąć _____

1. always _____ zawsze _____
2. any _____ żaden _____
3. because _____ ponieważ _____
4. been _____ nonexistent by itself _____
5. best _____ najlepszy _____
6. better _____ lepszy _____
7. both _____ oboje _____
8. bring _____ przynosić _____
9. buy _____ kupić _____
10. carry _____ nieść _____
11. clean _____ czysty _____
12. cut _____ krajać _____
13. does _____ robi _____
14. done _____ zrobione _____
15. drink _____ pić _____
16. fall _____ spadać _____
17. full _____ pełen _____
18. goes _____ idzie _____
19. got _____ dostał _____
20. grow _____ rosnąć _____
21. hold _____ trzymać _____
22. hot _____ gorący _____
23. hurt _____ boleć _____
24. its _____ tego _____

25. keep _____ trzymać _____
26. kind _____ miły _____
27. light _____ swiatło _____
28. live _____ żyć _____
29. myself _____ ja sam _____
30. off _____ nonexistent by itself _____
31. only _____ tylko _____
32. own _____ własny _____
33. pick _____ wybierać _____
34. pull _____ ciągnąć _____
35. read _____ czytać _____
36. right _____ prawy _____
37. seven _____ siedem _____
38. shall _____ będzie _____
39. sit _____ siedzieć _____
40. six _____ sześć _____
41. small _____ mały _____
42. start _____ zacząć _____
43. tell _____ opowiadać _____
44. ten _____ dziesięć _____
45. their _____ ich _____
46. these _____ te _____
47. those _____ tamte _____
48. today _____ dzisiaj _____
49. together _____ razem _____

DOLCH BASIC WORD LIST - POLISH

50. try _____ próbować _____

51. under _____ pod _____

52. upon _____ na _____

53. use _____ używać _____

54. warm _____ ciepły _____

55. wash _____ myć _____

56. well _____ dobrze _____

57. which _____ który _____

58. would _____ nonexistent by itself _____

59. write _____ pisać _____

60. draw _____ rysować _____

61. eight _____ osiem _____

DOLCH BASIC WORD LIST - PORTUGUESE

Pre-Primer

1. a __um, uma__
2. and __e__
3. big __grande__
4. blue __azul__
5. can __poder__
6. come __vir__
7. down __em baixo__
8. for __para (por)__
9. funny __engraçado__
10. get __ganhar__
11. go __ir__
12. green __verde__
13. have __ter__
14. help __ajudar__
15. here __aqui__
16. I __eu__
17. in __dentro (em)__
18. is __ser, estar__
19. it __ele, ela aquilo__
20. jump __pular__
21. little __pequeño__
22. look __olhar__
23. make __fazer__
24. me __mim__
25. my __meu (minha)__
26. not __não__
27. play __brincar, jogar__
28. red __vermelho__
29. ride __passeio__
30. run __correr__
31. said __disse__
32. saw __viu__ serra = the tool
33. see __ver__
34. the __o, a, os, as__
35. this __este, esta__
36. to __até para__
37. up __em cima__
38. want __desejar, querer__
39. we __nós__
40. with __com__
41. work __trabalho__
42. you __você__

Primer

1. all __todos__
2. am __sou (I am)__
3. are __são (they are) somos (we are)__
4. at __em__
5. away __ausente__
6. black __preto__
7. but __mas__
8. came __veio__
9. did __fiz, fez, fizeram__
10. do __fazer__
11. eat __comer__
12. fast __rápido__
13. find __achar__
14. good __bom, bôa__
15. he __ele__
16. laugh __riso__
17. like __gostar__
18. new __novo, nova__
19. no __não__
20. now __agora__
21. on __sobre__
22. one __um, uma__
23. out __fora__
24. please __por favor__
25. put __pôr__
26. ran __correu__
27. say __dizer__
28. she __ela__
29. so __então__
30. some __alguns, algumas__
31. stop __parar__
32. thank __agradecer__
33. that __aquele__
34. then __então__
35. they __eles__
36. three __três__
37. too __também__
38. two __dois__
39. was __eu fui, ele/ela foi__
40. went __foi__
41. what __o que__
42. where __onde__
43. white __branco__
44. will __será__
45. yellow __amarelo__
46. yes __sim__
47. your __seu, sua__

DOLCH BASIC WORD LIST - PORTUGUESE

First

1. about ___sobre___
2. after ___depois___
3. again ___outra vez___
4. an ___um, uma___
5. around ___arredor___
6. as ___como___
7. ask ___pedir___
8. ate ___comeu___
9. be ___ser, estar___
10. before ___antes___
11. brown ___castanho___
12. by ___por___
13. call ___chamar___
14. cold ___frio___
15. could ___poder___
16. can't ___não pode___
17. every ___cada, todo___
18. far ___longe___
19. first ___primeiro___
20. five ___cinco___

21. fly ___voar___
22. found ___achou___
23. four ___quatro___
24. from ___desde___
25. gave ___deu___
26. give ___dar___
27. going ___indo___
28. had ___teve___
29. has ___ter, ten___
30. her ___a, ela___
31. him ___o, ele___
32. his ___dele___
33. how ___como___
34. if ___se___
35. into ___em___
36. just ___somente, justo___
37. know ___saber___
38. let ___deixar___
39. long ___comprido___
40. made ___fez___
41. many ___muitos___

42. may ___poder___
43. much ___muito___
44. must ___deve___
45. never ___nunca___
46. of ___de___
47. old ___velho___
48. once ___certa vez___
49. open ___abrir___
50. or ___ou___
51. our ___nosso___
52. over ___sobre___
53. pretty ___lindo___
54. round ___redondo___
55. show ___mostrar___
56. sing ___cantar___
57. sleep ___dormir___
58. soon ___brevemente___
59. take ___levar___
60. them ___eles___
61. there ___ali___
62. think ___pensar___

63. us ___nós___
64. very ___muito___
65. walk ___andar___
66. were ___estavamos, eramos___
67. when ___quando___
68. who ___quem___
69. why ___por que?___
70. wish ___desejo___

DOLCH BASIC WORD LIST - PORTUGUESE

Second

1. always ___sempre___
2. any ___qualquer___
3. because ___porque___
4. been ___comó tem passado___
5. best ___o melhor___
6. better ___melhor___
7. both ___ambos___
8. bring ___trazer___
9. buy ___comprar___
10. carry ___carregar___
11. clean ___limpo___
12. cut ___cortar___
13. does ___faz___
14. done ___feito, fez___
15. drink ___beber___
16. fall ___cair___
17. full ___cheio___
18. goes ___vai___
19. got ___tem___
20. grow ___crescer___

21. hold ___segurar___
22. hot ___quente___
23. hurt ___machucar___
24. its ___é___
25. keep ___guardar___
26. kind ___tipo, bondoso___
27. light ___luz___
28. live ___viver___
29. myself ___eu mesmo___
30. off ___disligar___
31. only ___somente___
32. own ___próprio___
33. pick ___escolher___
34. pull ___puxar___
35. read ___ler___
36. right ___direito___
37. seven ___sete___
38. shall ___vai ser___
39. sit ___sentar-se___
40. six ___seis___
41. small ___pequeno___

42. start ___começo___
43. tell ___dizer___
44. ten ___dez___
45. their ___deles___
46. these ___êstes___
47. those ___aqueles, aquelas___
48. today ___hoje___
49. together ___juntos___
50. try ___tentar___
51. under ___em baixo___
52. upon ___sôbre___
53. use ___usar___
54. warm ___tépido, morno___
55. wash ___lavar___
56. well ___bem___
57. which ___qual___
58. would ___iria, faria___
59. write ___escrever___
60. draw ___desenhar___
61. eight ___oito___

DOLCH BASIC WORD LIST - RUSSIAN

Pre-Primer :

1. a —
2. and и
3. big большой
4. blue голубой
5. can могу
6. come приходить
7. down вниз
8. for за
9. funny смешной
10. get получать
11. go идти
12. green зелёный
13. have иметь
14. help помогать
15. here здесь
16. I я
17. in в
18. is есть
19. it это
20. jump прыгать
21. little маленький
22. look смотреть
23. make делать
24. please пожолуйста
25. my мой, моя, моё

26. not не
27. play играть
28. red красный
29. ride ехать верхом
30. run бежать
31. said сказал
32. saw видел
33. see видеть
34. the —
35. this этот, эта, это
36. to к
37. up вверх
38. want хотеть
39. we мы
40. with с
41. work работа
42. you ты, вы

Primer :

1. all все, всё
2. am —
3. are —
4. at возле, около
5. away прочь, от
6. black чёрный
7. but но

7. but но
8. came пришёл, (а)
9. did сделал, (а)
10. do делать
11. eat есть
12. fast быстро
13. find находить
14. good хорошо
15. he он
16. laugh смеяться
17. like нравиться
18. new новый
19. no нет
20. now сейчас
21. on на
22. one один
23. out из
24. please пожалуйста
25. put класть, положить
26. ran бежал
27. say сказать
28. she она
29. so так
30. some некоторые, (ая, ое)
31. stop остановить, (ся)

DOLCH BASIC WORD LIST - RUSSIAN

32. thank благодарить	9. be быть	34. if если
33. that тот, та	10. before перед, до	35. into в, внутрь
34. then тогда	11. brown коричневый	36. just только
35. they они	12. by около, у	37. know знать
36. three три	13. call звать	38. let позволять
37. too тоже	14. cold холодный	39. long длинный
38. two два	15. could мог, (могла)	40. made сделал, (а)
39. was был, (а, о)	16. can't не могу, (не может)	41. many много
40. went пошёл, ходил	17. every каждый	42. may можно
41. what что	18. far далеко	43. much много
42. where где	19. first первый	44. must должен
43. white белый	20. five пять	45. never никогда
44. will быть, (он будет, она будет)	21. fly летать	46. of от
45. yellow жёлтый	22. found нашёл, (нашла)	47. old старый
46. yes да	23. four четыре	48. once однажды
47. your твой твоя, твоё	24. from из	49. open открывать
First :	25. gave дал, (а)	50. or или
1. about о, об	26. give дать	51. our наш
2. after после	27. going идущий	52. over через
3. again снова	28. had имел, (а)	53. pretty красивый
4. an –	29. has иметь	54. round круглый
5. around вокруг	30. her её, ей	55. show показывать
6. as как	31. him ему	56. sing петь
7. ask спросить	32. his его	57. sleep спать
8. ate ел, (а) съел, (а)	33. how как	58. soon скоро

DOLCH BASIC WORD LIST - RUSSIAN

59. take взять, брать

60. them их

61. there вот, там

62. think думать

63. us нас, нам

64. very очень

65. walk ходить, гулять

66. were ты,мы, вы, они были

67. when когда

68. who кто

69. why почему

70. wish желать

Second :

1. always всегда

2. any каждый, любой

3. because потому что

4. been будучи

5. best лучший

6. better лучше

7. both обв, обе

8. bring приносить

9. buy покупать

10. carry нести

11. clean чистить

12. cut отрезать

13. does он,она, оно делает

14. done сделано, сделав

15. drink пить

16. fall падать

17. full полный

18. goes идти

19. got получил, (а)

20. grow расти

21. hold держать

22. hot горячий

23. hurt болеть

24. its этому, ей, его, свой, своя

25. keep держать

26. kind 1. добрый 2. сорт, род

27. light 1. лёгкий 2. свет

28. live жить

29. myself сам, (а)

30. off с, со, от

31. only только

32. own собственный

33. pick собирать

34. pull тянуть

35. read читать

36. right правый, правильно

37. seven семь

38. shall я, мы будем

39. sit сидеть

40. six шесть

41. small маленький

42. start начинать

43. tell рассказать

44. ten десять

45. their их

46. these эти

47. those тех, те

48. today сегодня

49. together вместе

50. try пытаться

51. under под

52. upon на

53. use пользоваться

54. warm тёплый

55. wash мыть

56. well хорошо

57. which который

58. would он,она,ты,вы, они бы, было бы

59. write писать

60. draw рисовать

61. eight восемь

DOLCH BASIC WORD LIST - SWEDISH

PRE-PRIMER

1.	a	en, ett	25.	my	min, mitt
2.	and	och	26.	not	inte
3.	big	stor	27.	play	leka
4.	blue	blå	28.	red	röd
5.	can	kan	29.	ride	rida, åka
6.	come	komma	30.	run	springa
7.	down	ner	31.	said	sade, sa
8.	for	för	32.	saw	såg
9.	funny	rolig	33.	see	se
10.	get	få	34.	the	
11.	go	gå	35.	this	denna, detta den, det
12.	green	grön	36.	to	till
13.	have	har, ha	37.	up	upp
14.	help	hjälp	38.	want	önska
15.	here	här	39.	we	vi
16.	I	jag	40.	with	med
17.	in	i, inne	41.	work	arbete
18.	is	är	42.	you	du
19.	it	den, det			
20.	jump	hoppa			
21.	little	liten			
22.	look	titta			
23.	make	göra			
24.	me	mig			

PRIMER

1.	all	alla
2.	am	är
3.	are	är
4.	at	vid, på, i
5.	away	iväg
6.	black	svart
7.	but	men
8.	came	kom
9.	did	gjorde
10.	do	gör, göra
11.	eat	äta
12.	fast	fort
13.	find	finna
14.	good	god, bra
15.	he	han
16.	laugh	skratta, scratt
17.	like	tycka, tycker
18.	new	ny
19.	no	nej
20.	now	nu
21.	on	på
22.	one	en, ett
23.	out	ut
24.	please	var snäll

DOLCH BASIC WORD LIST - SWEDISH

FIRST

25.	put	sätta, lägga	1.	about	omkring	
26.	ran	sprang	2.	after	efter	
27.	say	säga	3.	again	igen	
28.	she	hon	4.	an	en, ett	
29.	so	så	5.	around	omkring	
30.	some	några	6.	as	som	
31.	stop	stopp	7.	ask	fråga	
32.	thank	tacka, tack	8.	ate	åt	
33.	that	att	9.	be	vara	
34.	then	då	10.	before	före	
35.	they	de	11.	brown	brun	
36.	three	tre	12.	by	av, vid	
37.	too	också	13.	call	ringa, ropa	
38.	two	två	14.	cold	kall, kallt	
39.	was	var	15.	could	kunde	
40.	went	gick	16.	can't	kan inte	
41.	what	vad	17.	every	varje	
42.	where	var vart	18.	far	långt	
43.	white	vit	19.	first	först	
44.	will	vill	20.	five	fem	
45.	yellow	gul	21.	fly	flyga	
46.	yes	ja	22.	found	fann	
47.	your	din, ditt, dina	23.	four	fyra	
			24.	from	från	

25.	gave	gav
26.	give	giva, ge
27.	going	skall gå
28.	had	hade
29.	has	har
30.	her	henne, hennes
31.	him	honom
32.	his	hans
33.	how	hur
34.	if	om
35.	into	inuti
36.	just	bara, endast
37.	know	veta
38.	let	låt, låta
39.	long	lång
40.	made	gjorde
41.	many	många
42.	may	kan
43.	much	mycket
44.	must	måste
45.	never	aldrig
46.	of	av
47.	old	gammal
48.	once	en gång
49.	open	öppen, öppna

50. or _____ eller _____

51. our _____ vår _____

52. over _____ över _____

53. pretty _____ vacker _____

54. round _____ rund _____

55. show _____ visa _____

56. sing _____ sjunga _____

57. sleep _____ sova _____

58. soon _____ snart _____

59. take _____ ta _____

60. them _____ de _____

61. there _____ där _____

62. think _____ tänk _____

63. us _____ oss _____

64. very _____ varje _____

65. walk _____ promenera, gå _____

66. were _____ vore, blev _____

67. when _____ när _____

68. who _____ vem _____

69. why _____ varför _____

70. wish _____ önska _____

SECOND

1. always _____ alltid _____

2. any _____ någon _____

3. because _____ för att _____

4. been _____ varit _____

5. best _____ bäst _____

6. better _____ bättre _____

7. both _____ båda _____

8. bring _____ komma med _____

9. buy _____ köpa _____

10. carry _____ bära _____

11. clean _____ ren _____

12. cut _____ skära _____

13. does _____ gör _____

14. done _____ gjort _____

15. drink _____ dricka _____

16. fall _____ falla _____

17. full _____ full _____

18. goes _____ går _____

19. got _____ fått _____

20. grow _____ växa _____

21. hold _____ hålla _____

22. hot _____ het, varm _____

23. hurt _____ skadad _____

24. its _____ dess _____

25. keep _____ hålla _____

26. kind _____ vänlig _____

27. light _____ ljus _____

28. live _____ leva _____

29. myself _____ mig själv _____

30. off _____ av _____

31. only _____ endast _____

32. own _____ egen, äga _____

33. pick _____ plocka _____

34. pull _____ draga _____

35. read _____ läsa _____

36. right _____ rätt, höger _____

37. seven _____ sju _____

38. shall _____ skall _____

39. sit _____ sitt, sitta _____

40. six _____ sex _____

41. small _____ liten _____

42. start _____ börja _____

43. tell _____ berätta _____

44. ten _____ tio _____

45. their _____ deras _____

46. these _____ dess de här _____

47. those _____ dessa _____

48. today _____ idag _____

49. together _____ tillsammans _____

50. try _____försöka_____

51. under _____under_____

52. upon _____på_____

53. use _____använda_____

54. warm _____varm_____

55. wash _____tväta_____

56. well _____väl bra_____

57. which _____vilken_____

58. would _____skulle, kunde_____

59. write _____skriva_____

60. draw _____rita_____

61. eight _____åtta_____

DOLCH BASIC WORD LIST - THAI

Pre-Primer :

1. a	-	26. not	ไม่
2. and	และ	27. play	เล่น
3. big	ใหญ่	28. red	สีแดง
4. blue	สีน้ำเงิน	29. ride	ขี่
5. can	กระป๋อง	30. run	วิ่ง
6. come	มา	31. said	ได้บอก, ได้พูด
7. down	ลง	32. saw	ได้เห็น
8. for	สำหรับ	33. see	เห็น
9. funny	ตลก, น่าขัน	34. the	-
10. get	ได้รับ	35. this	นี้
11. go	ไป	36. to	ถึง
12. green	สีเขียว	37. up	ชี้ไป, ข้างบน
13. have	มี	38. want	ต้องการ
14. help	ช่วยเหลือ	39. we	พวกเรา
15. here	ที่นี่	40. with	ด้วย, กับ
16. I	ฉัน	41. work	ทำงาน
17. in	ใน	42. you	คุณ
18. is	เป็น		
19. it	มัน	**Primer :**	
20. jump	กระโดด	1. all	ทั้งหมด
21. little	เล็กน้อย	2. am	เป็น
22. look	มองดู	3. are	เป็น
23. make	ทำ	4. at	ที่
24. please	กรุณา	5. away	ไกลออกไป
25. my	ของฉัน	6. black	สีดำ
		7. but	แต่

7. but	แต่
8. came	มาแล้ว
9. did	ได้ทำ
10. do	ทำ
11. eat	กิน
12. fast	เร็ว
13. find	เจอ, หา, พบ
14. good	ดี
15. he	เขา (ชาย)
16. laugh	หัวเราะ
17. like	ชอบ
18. new	ใหม่
19. no	ไม่
20. now	เดี๋ยวนี้
21. on	บน
22. one	หนึ่ง
23. out	ออก, ข้างนอก
24. please	กรุณา
25. put	วาง, ใส่
26. ran	ได้วิ่ง
27. say	บอก, พูด
28. she	เขา (ผู้หญิง)
29. so	ดังนั้น
30. some	บางอัน
31. stop	หยุด

DOLCH BASIC WORD LIST - THAI

32.	thank	ขอบคุณ	9.	be	เป็น	34. if	ถ้า
33.	that	นั้น , สิ่งนั้น	10.	before	ก่อน	35. into	ข้างใน
34.	then	เวลานั้น	11.	brown	สีน้ำตาล	36. just	เพียง
35.	they	พวกเขา	12.	by	โดย	37. know	ทราบ , รู้
36.	three	สาม	13.	call	เรียก	38. let	ให้
37.	too	ด้วย	14.	cold	หนาว	39. long	ยาว , นาน
38.	two	สอง	15.	could	สามารถ , ทำได้	40. made	ได้ทำ
39.	was	เป็น	16.	can't	ทำไม่ได้	41. many	มาก , จำนวนมาก
40.	went	ได้ไป	17.	every	ทุก ๆ	42. may	อาจจะ
41.	what	อะไร	18.	far	ไกล	43. much	มาก
42.	where	ที่ไหน	19.	first	ครั้งแรก, ที่หนึ่ง	44. must	ต้อง
43.	white	สีขาว	20.	five	ห้า	45. never	ไม่เคย
44.	will	จะ	21.	fly	บิน	46. of	ของ
45.	yellow	สีเหลือง	22.	found	ได้พบ	47. old	แก่ , เก่า
46.	yes	ใช่, ค่ะ , ครับ.	23.	four	สี่	48. once	ครั้งหนึ่ง
47.	your	ของคุณ	24.	from	จาก	49. open	เปิด
First :			25.	gave	ได้ให้	50. or	หรือ
1.	about	เกี่ยวกับ	26.	give	ให้	51. our	ของเรา
2.	after	หลังจาก	27.	going	กำลังไป	52. over	ข้างบน
3.	again	อีกที	28.	had	เคยมี	53. pretty	สวย
4.	an	-	29.	has	มี	54. round	กลม
5.	around	รอบ ๆ	30.	her	ของเขา (ผู้หญิง)	55. show	แสดง
6.	as	เหมือนกับ	31.	him	เขา (ผู้ชาย)	56. sing	ร้องเพลง
7.	ask	ขอ, ถาม	32.	his	ของเขา (ผู้ชาย)	57. sleep	นอนหลับ
8.	ate	ได้กินแล้ว	33.	how	อย่างไร	58. soon	อีกไม่นาน

DOLCH BASIC WORD LIST - THAI

59.	take	เอาไป	13.	does	ทำ	38.	shall	จะ
60.	them	พวกเขา	14.	done	ทำเสร็จ	39.	sit	นั่ง
61.	there	ที่นั่น	15.	drink	ดื่ม	40.	six	หก
62.	think	คิด	16.	fall	ตก	41.	small	เล็ก
63.	us	พวกเรา	17.	full	เต็ม	42.	start	เริ่ม
64.	very	มาก	18.	goes	ไป	43.	tell	บอก
65.	walk	เดิน	19.	got	ได้แล้ว	44.	ten	สิบ
66.	were	เป็น,เคยเป็น	20.	grow	เติบโต,ปลูก	45.	their	ของเขา
67.	when	เมื่อ	21.	hold	จับ,ถือ	46.	these	อันเหล่านี้
68.	who	ใคร	22.	hot	ร้อน	47.	those	อันเหล่านั้น
69.	why	ทำไม	23.	hurt	เจ็บ	48.	today	วันนี้
70.	wish	ประสงค์,ปรารถนา	24.	its	ของมัน	49.	together	ด้วยกัน
Second :			25.	keep	เก็บ	50.	try	พยายาม
1.	always	เสมอ	26.	kind	ชนิด,แบบ	51.	under	ข้างใต้
2.	any	อันไหนก็ได้	27.	light	แสง	52.	upon	ข้างบน
3.	because	เพราะว่า	28.	live	อยู่อาศัย	53.	use	ใช้
4.	been	เป็น	29.	myself	ตัวฉันเอง	54.	warm	อบอุ่น
5.	best	ดีที่สุด	30.	off	ปิด,ถอด	55.	wash	ล้าง
6.	better	ดีกว่า,ดีขึ้น	31.	only	เพียง	56.	well	สบายดี
7.	both	ทั้งสอง	32.	own	เป็นเจ้าของ	57.	which	อันไหน
8.	bring	เอามา	33.	pick	เก็บ,เลือก	58.	would	จะ
9.	buy	ซื้อ	34.	pull	ดึง	59.	write	เขียน
10.	carry	ถือ	35.	read	อ่าน	60.	draw	วาดภาพ
11.	clean	สะอาด	36.	right	ถูกต้อง,ขวา	61.	eight	แปด
12.	cut	ตัด	37.	seven	เจ็ด			